Contents

Chapter 1: Early Days............................ 1
Chapter 2: HMS *Edinburgh*..................... 11
Chapter 3: Convoy QP11......................... 33
Chapter 4: Castaways in Arctic Russia 52
Chapter 5: Homeward Bound.................... 66
Chapter 6: D.E.M.S................................ 81
Chapter 7: Abroad Again........................ 102
Chapter 8: Calcutta............................. 123
Chapter 9: Mynah Birds and Monkeys............ 140
Chapter 10: Home Again........................ 150

Illustrations

Convoy QP11 to Iceland 38/39

Photographs

HMS Edinburgh. 91
Captain Faulkner & Admiral Bonham-Carter 91
Foc'sle Ice, H.M.S. Edinburgh 92
Hermann Shoemann on fire and sinking 92
H.M.S. Harrier taking Edinburgh survivors. 93
Greenwich College 93
Painted Hall, Greenwich College. 94

Chapter 1

Early Days

W hen World War Two broke out in September 1939, I was 19 years old and living in Bangor, Co. Down.
The rumblings and war clouds had been gathering for a number of years. In fact, when I left school at 18, many of my contemporaries were joining the O.T.C. (Officer Training Corps) at Queens University, Belfast. This was an organisation for training officer cadets for the British Army. Since I had always been interested in the sea, ships and anything maritime, I was more attracted to training for the Royal Navy than going in for the Army.

Norman Sparksman

At that time the Navy had a training ship called H.M.S. *Caroline* moored in Belfast docks, which was the headquarters of the R.N.V.R. (Royal Naval Volunteer Reserve). I, along with a number of my friends in Ballyholme Yacht Club, applied to the British Admiralty for membership of the R.N.V.R. in Belfast. In those days it was not easy to get in and was considered something of an honour to be accepted. One had to sit a written examination in seamanship, navigation, etc. and pass through an interview board, satisfying them that one had a fairly wide knowledge of the sea, boat handling, navigation and maritime matters generally. There were always more applicants than vacancies, so there was keen competition for acceptance. Of the five of us who applied together, one failed the written examination, one failed the interview board and three (including myself) passed through both. We had been accepted, subject to medical examination. It was a number of weeks before we were called back for the medical, and in the meantime there was great jubilation amongst the three of us who had been accepted into the R.N.V.R. Eventually we were called back to H.M.S. *Caroline* for the medical. My two friends passed the medical and I failed the eyesight test. I was shattered by this as I had been looking forward to starting my naval training having passed through all of the tests so far, including the remainder of the medical. At the time I did not know it but this was the first of many setbacks throughout my life caused by my defective eyesight. Nowadays the mild myopia from which I suffered could be compensated for by contact lenses but such innovations were unheard of at that time.

By the time the war started in September 1939, my friends who had joined the R.N.V.R. were called up. Thinking that in wartime the powers that be would not be so fussy about slight short-sightedness, I reapplied for the R.N.V.R. but again without success for the same reason.

Jottings of a Young Sailor

The R.N.V.R was a Naval Officer reserve. Still wanting to go to sea, I thought that if they would not take me as an officer, was there any other capacity in which I could be accepted? With this thought in mind, I went to the Naval recruiting office in Belfast. When the war commenced, conscription was introduced in Great Britain and all men not in reserved occupations were called up for service in the armed forces for the duration of the war. Reserved occupations included police, firemen, munitions workers and others who worked in jobs which were essential to the war effort. There was no conscription in Northern Ireland and anyone who joined the forces volunteered by going to the recruiting offices. Thus I found myself at the Naval Recruiting office, enquiring how I could get to sea despite my eyesight problem. To my surprise I was welcomed with open arms and told I could join as a Telegraphist; so this I promptly did. I signed up and was sent home to await being called up. Again, somewhat surprisingly, I waited for nearly two years!

Eventually the call came, and on 18th June 1941 I went off in charge of four other recruits heading for H.M.S. *Impregnable*, which was a signals training school in Devonport.

The journey to Devonport was interminable. Flying was not an option in those days. Passenger-carrying aeroplanes were still rare. We travelled by overnight boat from Belfast to Heysham in Lancashire and thence by train (which seemed to stop at every hamlet on the way) to Devonport, which was one of the three Naval Divisional Ports (the others being Portsmouth and Chatham). The journey took over 24 hours and I remember arriving at the gates of H.M.S. *Impregnable* late in the evening with my five companions, not knowing what to expect when we entered.

H.M.S. *Impregnable* was a former prison on the outskirts of Devonport which had been converted into a naval barracks and signals training school. The main prison building was on top of a small hill. Additional accommodation in the form of wooden huts had been added in the grounds inside the perimeter fence which surrounded the site around the bottom of the hill. We were soon to find that there was an ammunition factory around the bottom of the hill and the hill itself had tunnels and caverns burrowed into it for the storage of ammunition. So we were in the position of sitting on top of an ammunition dump which was surrounded by an ammunition factory. The thought of this situation added impetus to our efforts on fire-fighting duty during the many German air raids encountered during our stay at this location.

Entering the gates of this formidable-looking establishment with some trepidation, we reported to the sentry on duty, who handed us over to the duty Petty Officer. We were a little surprised at the cordial welcome he gave us. Realising that we were somewhat weary after a long, tiring journey from Northern Ireland, he first ushered us into the main mess hall of the prison and arranged a meal for us, following which we were allocated a hut to sleep for the night. The huts which provided the sleeping accommodation held about 10 or 12 double bunks, one above the other, and we soon found the huts were full of newly arrived recruits looking just as bewildered by it all as we felt.

Next morning it was of some comfort to us to find that, far from being one or two isolated new recruits amongst a crowd of seasoned sailors, many of the occupants were new recruits like ourselves. Although the daily routine was run in the fashion of a ship, it was a training establishment and run as a school during the day. The newcomers were divided into classes; those of us like me who were to be Telegraphists went off to telegraphy classes and others who were to be Signallers went to their specialist classes. The 'teachers' were mostly last-war Chief Petty Officers who really 'knew their stuff' as far as telegraphy and naval routine were concerned.

Jottings of a Young Sailor

The telegraphy classes were not without their humorous side as we settled down to the serious business of learning Morse code and the technicalities of sending radio messages from ship to ship.

The classes consisted of about 20 trainees sitting at individual desks in a hut. Each operator represented a ship with its own individual call sign. The Chief Petty Officer instructor sat at a desk in the middle of the room and represented the Commander-in-Chief, through whom radio messages went to and from the 'Admiralty'. Some of the messages were quite complicated, in the sense that they might be sent to a particular ship via the Commander-in-Chief and repeated to several other ships for information. We had to learn that there had to be immediate official responses to these messages in the correct form. Bear in mind that we were all sitting at our Morse keys wearing headphones, listening intently to the Morse messages buzzing in our ears in case our own ship's call sign came over. The room was completely silent apart from the occasional tapping of Morse keys. Woe betide the ship that did not respond, or responded without the required alacrity. The silence would suddenly be shattered by the instructor (Commander-in-Chief) taking off his headphones and enquiring in a thunderous voice, and with a string of oaths and colourful language, whether such-and-such a ship had really sunk without trace or merely that all the telegraphists on board had fallen asleep!!

As it turned out, telegraphists falling asleep at their keys became something of a problem for the Training Commander in charge of this Signals School. It was in the months of June and July, 1941, when there was a particularly hot summer in the south of England. Also, this was a time when German air raid blitzes were at their height, especially on strategic targets like Naval Bases and dockyards, to say nothing of ammunition factories and dumps! We found that as soon as dusk fell, the bombers came in droves and stayed most of the night, every night. The pattern was to bomb in waves. The first wave would drop incendiaries and the second high explosive bombs. We soon found we were learning more about fire-fighting than about telegraphy. The combination of loss of sleep by being up all night fire-fighting most nights and sitting during the day with headphones on in huts overheated by the hot sun, did indeed result in many of us falling asleep in the classrooms. At the height of the blitzes, classroom work during the day was eventually cancelled altogether to allow us to sleep so that we would be fresh enough to fight fires at night. When the nightly bombing became less intense, we reverted to the more normal routine of sleeping at night and doing our classroom telegraphy during the daytime.

I had gone about halfway through the Telegraphist's course and become quite proficient at using the Morse key and sending and receiving messages in the various formats used by the Navy. Also by this time, I had become quite at home with Navy life and its sometimes odd customs. Although a shore training establishment, H.M.S. *Impregnable* was run as a ship, with various divisions which were paraded every morning and evening, each division in charge of a Divisional Officer. Most of these officers were R.N.V.R., but the Training Commander and Captain were R.N. For the purposes of assessment, all recruits were sooner or later interviewed by their Divisional Officer. When my turn came, I was asked if I wanted to be considered for a commission (i.e. promoted to commissioned rank, becoming an officer). When I said, 'Yes, provided I can go to sea,' my officer said, 'Do you really want to become the lowest form of animal life in the Navy by becoming a Sub-Lieutenant?'

In the event I was started on the rather lengthy process of officer training. I would have to stop my telegraphy training, transfer to seaman class and train as a Seaman, put in at least six months' sea time on the lower deck on active service, pass through a selection board presided over by my seagoing Captain, then come ashore and pass through three different training schools and finally, pass through an Admiralty selection board. If I cleared all of these hurdles I would be commissioned with the rank of Sub-Lieutenant. At the time my main concern was that I wanted to go to sea and knowing that one of the few openings in the Navy for someone with poor eyesight was as a telegraphist, I enquired whether I could still go to sea if promoted to officer rank. I was told yes, I would be able to find some category which would give me a seagoing job. With this assurance, I agreed to 'go for it', and so I became what was known as a C.W. candidate along with a number of other ratings. A C.W. file on me was started; this file followed me forever afterwards during my 'wanderings' through the Navy. (The 'C.W.' came from the Admiralty Department of Commissions and Warrants which was the section of the Navy which dealt with such matters.) As C.W. candidates, we were in all other respects no different from our other shipmates and carried the same ranks of Ordinary Seaman, Able Seaman, Leading Seaman, or whatever. Of course, our shipmates, with typical naval humour, always referred to us as W.C. candidates.

On 30th August 1941, I departed H.M.S. *Impregnable* and transferred to H.M.S. *Raleigh*, also in Devonport, which was a Seaman training school. Here I joined large numbers of other recruits coming into the Navy for the first time to be trained as seamen. A number of my new-found friends from *Impregnable*, also C.W. candidates, went with me to *Raleigh*, so at least there was someone I knew in amongst the throng of somewhat bewildered newcomers. We all quickly settled down to life on the new 'ship' and made many new friends. I made some friends here who were to stay with me through many moves and eventually were to serve with me at sea on the same ship.

Norman Sparksman

The course at *Raleigh* took several months, learning the intricacies of seamanship: ropes and splices, anchors and chains, shipboard life etc. I enjoyed the classes, which were conducted mostly by retired last-war Chief Petty Officers brought back as instructors. These fellows really knew their stuff, having spent a lifetime in the Navy. Not only did they have (so it seemed to us) a vast knowledge of the sea and ships but they were excellent instructors as well. A lot of the instruction was of a practical nature and the 'Chiefies', as we called them, looked with great patience and a kind of fatherly benevolence on our feeble efforts to act and behave like seamen. Also, they mostly had a great sense of humour. The classes were usually made up of about twenty recruits, and I remember one day early in the course when the C.P.O. was still trying to remember each of our names. He had us lined up on the parade ground and was getting us to call out our names in turn. The chap beside me, a rather 'toffee-nosed' character, had the somewhat unusual and high-sounding name of Sidebottom, which he pronounced 'SeedyboTOM', with the emphasis on the last syllable. When the instructor heard this he exclaimed 'What! How'd you spell that?' The unfortunate guy spelled it out: 'S-i-d-e-b-o-t-t-o-m.' 'Oh,' said the instructor, 'Sidebottom. Let's just call you Slantarse.' The nickname stayed with him for the rest of his life in the Navy. On another occasion, during a class on the characteristics of different kinds of wood, the instructor picked up a sample and declared, in a broad cockney accent, 'Now, this 'ere's a piece of teak. Very strong and durable wood, teak, used for decking on ships and for making piles for piers, and when I says piles for piers I does *not* mean 'emmoroids for the aristocracy!'

Eventually, on 6th October 1941, after a series of examinations and practical tests, we passed out and were considered fit to be let loose on one of His Majesty's ships as Ordinary Seamen.

Jottings of a Young Sailor

Once again we were on the move. This time to be drafted to H.M.S. *Drake* in Devonport, which was the main Naval Barracks. This was a huge establishment holding thousands and which was more like a transit camp. There were three of these barracks: one each at Chatham, Portsmouth and Devonport. All lower deck ratings belonged and were based permanently at one or other of these 'depots'. The inhabitants of these barracks were ratings of various kinds who were temporarily on passage from one ship to another. Quite frequently, as I was to find out later, the ship they had been on had been sunk in action and they had been sent back to barracks to await posting to another ship.

With such large numbers of men coming and going, it was like living in a large town whose population was constantly changing. The accommodation was constantly overcrowded and there always seemed to be more coming in than going out. One remedy used to cope with this situation, and which no one objected to, was to send people on leave unless drafting to another ship was imminent. This is what happened to me. After a short time in barracks I was sent on 'indefinite' leave to await posting.

One of the problems in a barracks such as this was to keep the men occupied. In the Navy one could never be seen to be unoccupied. It used to amuse us to see the lengths that were taken to keep people occupied. Unlike a training establishment where people were occupied going to classes, in a barracks there was little to do other than keep the place clean – and it didn't need an army to do that. So long as you were seen to be occupied, it mattered not if you were doing nothing, and one soon became very adept at doing nothing with great efficiency, vigour and dedication. We were detailed each morning to all kinds of odd jobs just to keep us occupied.

One occasion comes to mind. I was detailed to spend the morning, along with a couple of other lads, picking up and disposing of all the cigarette butts which were disfiguring the ground immediately outside the main entrance to the barracks. To accomplish this mammoth task, of course we had to leave the ship and go 'ashore', so had to have passes to get through the Guard Room on the way out. Also, because we were going ashore, we had to be properly dressed in going-ashore clothes. Once outside at our appointed place of duty, we conscientiously applied ourselves to 'doing nothing'. How many butts can you pick up in a whole morning?! During the course of this inspiring occupation we got chatting among the three of us. We had never met before and found we were indeed a motley crew. I was an insurance clerk, one man was a trainee barrister and the other was a very young film actor by the name of Michael Redgrave. The latter was to become much better known for his exploits on the silver screen after the war. When 'hands to dinner' was piped at lunch time we stopped doing what we were doing (whether it was finished or not!) because being now 'off watch', it was all right to be seen doing nothing. We went back on board through the Guard Room to our respective messes. I never saw my two companions again as I was sent home on leave the next day to await posting.

Chapter 2
H.M.S. Edinburgh

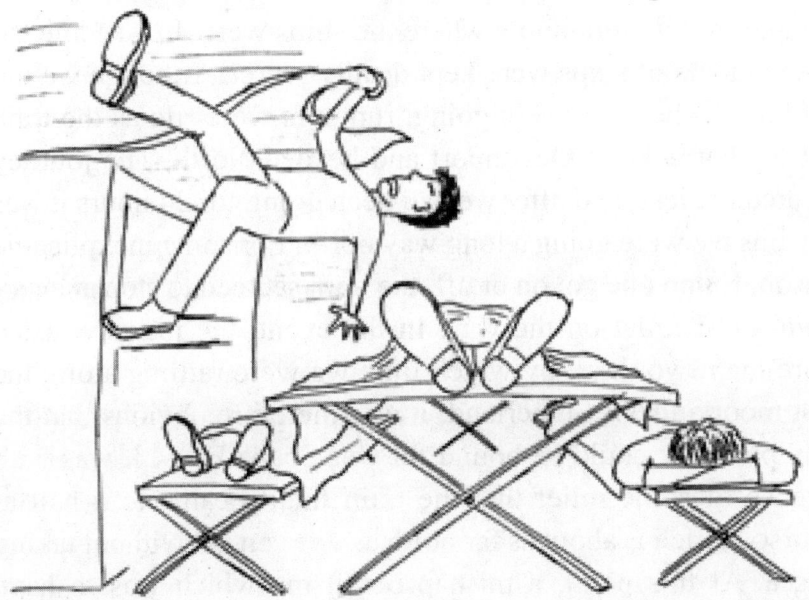

My leave lasted a fortnight, and I had returned to H.M.S. *Drake* but a few days when the expected 'chitty' arrived and I was posted to H.M.S. *Edinburgh*. Great excitement, jubilation and expectation, because not only was this a 'big' ship, one of the latest 10,000 ton heavy cruisers, but also quite a number of my friends who had been in training in the early days at H.M.S. *Impregnable* were also drafted to the same ship. We were amongst a draft of perhaps 10 ratings, mostly recruits going to *Edinburgh*. However, there were something like 500 other ratings of various ranks in the same draft going to other ships in the Home Fleet, which at the time was based mostly at Scapa Flow in the Orkney Isles and Valfjord in Iceland. There was such a large body of men going north to Scapa that a special troop train was laid on. This special train was backed into a siding actually inside the barracks at H.M.S. *Drake*, so there was no problem getting from our billets to the train. There were no passengers other than Naval personnel. At the time, no one knew where we were going. We knew which ships we were going to but did not know where the ships were. In wartime the whereabouts of ships were kept deadly secret. Although we did not know where we were going, rumours were rife as the train left the barracks in Devonport and headed North. The journey seemed endless, and after we had been going for 24 hours it was obvious we were going a long way north. For some inexplicable reason, for no one got on or off, the train seemed to stop at every town and hamlet on the way. In the event, the journey lasted more than two days, by which time we were rattling along the vast moorlands of Sutherland; it was therefore obvious that the only place we could be bound for was Scapa Flow. It was with a sense of some relief that the train finally came to a halt at Thurso, which is about as far north as one can get without taking to sea. At this point, a mishap befell me which was to have odd consequences.

One of the first things one learns early in Service life is to look after one's personal baggage, because thieves abound and it is the easiest thing in the world to 'lose' things. On the way up from Devonport all of my baggage except my gas mask was packed in my kit bag, which had a padlock on it. My gas mask I managed to keep in sight all the way to Thurso. When preparing to leave the train, I turned to get my kit bag off the overhead luggage rack, and when I turned round my gas mask was gone. Plenty of gas masks around, but with everyone in

Jottings of a Young Sailor

the same uniform carrying the same gas masks, which one was mine? I never recovered it.

We disembarked from the train and boarded a ferry to take us to Scapa Flow, where we boarded the old battleship *Royal Oak*, which had been torpedoed by a U-boat and was sitting on the bottom, quite upright with her upper works well clear of the water. She was being used as a transit ship where personnel were temporarily boarded while waiting to board the ships to which they had been drafted. I had been drafted to *Edinburgh* but by the time I arrived at Scapa, she had gone to sea and was presently located at Vaalfjord in Iceland and not likely to return to Scapa for some time. Arrangements were therefore made for me to take passage to Iceland in the cruiser *Cumberland*, one of the three-funnelled County Class cruisers armed with 8-inch guns. This was an uneventful passage which took about two or three days. Arriving in Vaalfjord I eventually caught up with *Edinburgh* and boarded the ship which was to be my home while I completed the sea time which was to be part of my officer training.

I was allocated to fo'c'sle division which is in the forward part of the ship and made my way to the mess deck to get settled in. In the meantime, I had reported the loss of my gas mask and was immediately put on a charge to appear at 'Commander's defaulters' the following morning. At defaulters I told my story about the missing gas mask and considered myself lucky not to be punished for losing it. The Commander merely asked the Petty Officer to see if he could find another one for me, and let me off with a caution about being careful to take proper care of service property issued to me in future. The odd outcome was that, despite the fact that a fighting ship – especially a large one like a cruiser – is a completely self-contained unit with spare parts for practically everything on board, from guns to pencils, they were never able to produce a gas mask for me in all the time I was at sea on active service and might have wanted one. I was never able to obtain another gas mask until long after having been in action and having had my ship sunk under me and been returned to the U.K. as a survivor!

It was now November 1941. I was 21 years old and about to begin what I afterwards considered to be the best part of my education. Joining the ship's company of a fighting ship on active service in wartime was an eye-opener. I had always imagined the Navy as a rather stuffy, hidebound service, peopled by long-serving professionals. In fact, the long-serving professionals were very much in the minority. The majority of the ship's company, which numbered about 700 officers and men, were, like myself, 'Hostilities Only' personnel. True, some of the senior officers, including the Captain, and most of the Chief Petty Officers, were long-serving career officers but the remainder were in for wartime service only.

I soon found that my 'mates' on the mess deck came from all walks of life. There were trainee barristers, bank clerks, insurance officials, plumbers, architects and many more. One of my best friends was a zoo keeper. Religions were just as varied; Christians, Jews, Agnostics; and characters the same; good characters, bad characters. Living in close company on the mess decks and sharing the trials and tribulations of shipboard life on active service, one got to know them all, and even if you did not like someone you learned to live with them. There were occasional personality clashes and fist fights when tempers flared but the strongest feeling of all, which seemed to override all else, was a sort of camaraderie and respect, where a helping hand was always given to another shipmate when it was needed, whether it be in the mess deck, on deck in bad weather or in action amidst torpedo and shell. I think it came from the realisation that ultimately our welfare and very lives depended on each of us doing his individual job well. Although there was plenty of banter from the old hands about the feeble efforts of us rookies, there was also instruction, guidance and assistance freely given where needed. The Chief Petty Officers, or 'Chiefies' as they were called, once they were satisfied that we had accepted the stern Naval discipline and were no longer inclined to rebel against it, were helpful in their instruction and kept a fatherly eye on our activities.

On joining the ship, newcomers came in at the bottom end of the hierarchy. You got the worst and dirtiest jobs to do. You did not get a locker to hold your gear but had to use your kitbag. You did not get to sling your hammock in the mess deck because it was full. You had to find any other odd corner in the ship to 'sling'. The only place I could find was in a place called the capstan engine flat. This was a sort of engine room immediately under the fo'c'sle deck where the huge electric engines which drove the capstans for winding the anchor cables were housed. At first I wondered why so few hammocks were slung here. When we went to sea I was soon to find out. These engines were only used when the ship was entering or leaving harbour but if this happened to be in the middle of the night, when you might be off watch and asleep, you had to get up, unsling your hammock and get out of the way so that the engine crew could operate the engines. If you didn't get out of the way they operated them anyway, and the noise of the engines, together with the grinding and rattling of the heavy anchor cables on the fo'c'sle deck above, put sleep out of the question.

The operational area in which the ship was working was mostly north of the Arctic Circle, either on patrol in the Denmark Straits between Iceland and Greenland or escorting convoys to Archangel or Murmansk. This produced problems of cold. One of these problems manifested itself in the capstan engine flat. The deck head in this flat was immediately underneath the open fo'c'sle, and as soon as the ship went north of the Arctic Circle, the deck head temperature dropped permanently below freezing point. The consequence of this was that the water vapour in the atmosphere froze onto the deck head and formed a thin layer of ice which continually grew while we were in northern latitudes. This caused no problems when it was frozen but when the ship returned below the Arctic Circle again, the ice started to melt. By this time it might be up to two inches thick. As the ship rolled, the ice, which had a thin layer of water between it and the deck head, started to slide from side to side, and it was only a matter of time before a large, wet slab would become detached and splash down to the deck below. This was somewhat disconcerting if you happened to be asleep in your hammock and got in the path of the falling ice. Those of us who slept in this area took to wearing our oilskin coats while asleep to combat the problem. Luckily, the problem only arose when the ship was heading south from the cold northern latitudes to the relatively warmer area below the Arctic Circle. Similarly, in the mess decks below, which were adjacent to the side of the ship, when the ice on the inside of the ship melted, large slabs would slide onto the deck and we would be paddling around in our sea boots for hours, mopping up the mixture of ice and water to get the mess deck dry enough to live in.

Life at sea consisted mainly of long periods of sheer boredom punctuated by short periods of intense activity. Cruisers spend a lot of time at sea as opposed to battleships, which spend most of their time in harbour. We would leave Scapa Flow to go on a fortnight's patrol in the Denmark Straits, and on return would find the same battleships at anchor in the same spot as when we left. There was always a lot of banter between the cruiser and battleship crews when on shore leave in Scapa, the cruiser boys complaining they were doing all the work while the battleship boys enjoyed harbour routine all the time. It was often chided that if the battleships didn't soon go to sea they would go aground on their own empty milk tins!

It was in the nature of naval warfare at the time that battleships seldom put to sea. As capital ships, their mere presence in an area was a threat, meant to counter a similar threat from the other side. The H.M.S. *King George IV* and H.M.S. *Hood*, anchored in Scapa Flow, countered the threat of the German battleship *Tirpitz*, anchored in the Norwegian fjords. If there was any reported movement of the *Tirpitz* (or any other German ships), it was the cruisers' job to put to sea and try to locate the enemy. I well remember one occasion when we had just dropped anchor in Scapa after a patrol in the miserable weather off Greenland, and were looking forward to some rest in harbour for a few days. A few hours after arriving in harbour, we suddenly weighed anchor and left again. It was the practice that we were never told where we were going until outside harbour. On this occasion the Captain came on the ship's intercom and announced that there was a rumour that the *Tirpitz* had left harbour and we were going out to look for her. A great groan went up and some wag muttered, 'I hope to God we never find her!' In the event, the rumour was countermanded a few hours after we left, so we turned tail and headed back to Scapa as fast as we had left.

The presence of the German capital ships in the Norwegian fjords posed a threat to Allied shipping in the Atlantic, and a constant watch was kept on the exit routes from Norway to the Atlantic. These exit routes were via the North Sea between Norway and Scotland or between Scotland and Iceland; through the English Channel; or via the Denmark Straits between Iceland and Greenland. The last route was in the remotest area and most difficult to cover, and was thus considered the most likely route to be followed by any of the enemy ships trying to break into the Atlantic. Patrolling the Denmark Straits was one of the two main tasks carried out by H.M.S. *Edinburgh*. A patrol would normally last a fortnight, after which we would return to our base in Iceland for a few days' rest pending our next assignment, which might be another similar patrol or our second main task of escorting a convoy to North Russia. These Denmark Straits' patrols were usually carried out by two cruisers, and the ship normally accompanying us was H.M.S. *Cumberland*, the ship in which I had taken passage from Scapa to Iceland. Each ship would steam slowly across the Straits, starting from opposite sides, meeting and passing in the middle. Visibility most of the time was very poor, and in winter it was perpetually dark, as we were above the Arctic Circle. This meant that the only way we could 'see' was with our radar, and the screens were carefully and constantly scanned. The Denmark Straits are about 200 miles wide, and every 24 hours or so the two ships would approach each other in the middle and pick one another up on their radar. All that could be seen was another sizeable ship; the chances were it was the other patrolling cruiser, but it just could be an enemy ship trying to slip through the straits. The consequence was that ACTION STATIONS was sounded on both ships, gun crews closed up, guns loaded. In our case we had twelve 6-inch guns loaded and the gunnery director sitting with his finger on the trigger, waiting to fire if the ship gradually emerging out of the Arctic mist and darkness did not immediately flash the identification signal on its signal lamp. There was always the uneasy feeling of knowing that the crew of the *Cumberland* were doing exactly the same as us and had their eight 8-inch guns trained on us and ready to fire.

The two signallers having saved us all from being blown to kingdom-come, the two ships pass and shipboard life returns to more peaceful normality until we meet again on the return crossing. This sequence of events, which tends to become a little tiresome, repeats itself for the duration of the patrol every time the two ships meet in the middle of the straits.

Some time after the Japanese attack on Pearl Harbor, which brought America into the war, an American fleet hitherto never seen in European waters was sent to Europe. Their aid was sorely needed, as up until then the war at sea on many fronts – the Atlantic, the Mediterranean, the North sea, and the Arctic – had been fought solely by the Royal Navy, aided by small contingents of Allied forces from France, Norway etc.

The American fleet was a large one, consisting of several battleships and aircraft carriers escorted by squadrons of cruisers and destroyers. It crossed the Atlantic and headed for Scapa Flow, which was the main base for the British Home Fleet. The *Edinburgh* was given the job of rendezvousing with the American fleet 300 miles or so out in the Western Approaches and escorting them to Scapa. This job came as a pleasant change from our usual boring role of patrols and convoy work. The day we met this American fleet is for ever etched in my memory. It had been blowing a gale in the Atlantic for a week, and huge seas had built up. Fifty- or 60-foot waves are not uncommon and, as often happens with Atlantic gales, when they pass the weather clears and there is brilliant sunshine, although there is still a high wind. When we met the fleet, they were steaming along slowly in formation and presented a magnificent sight in the rough sea. The battleships were just ploughing through the seas in clouds of spray which at times completely hid them from view. The aircraft carriers were riding over the tops of the waves and then dipping the forward end of their flight decks down into the troughs. Coming up on the next wave, they would scoop up hundreds of gallons of water onto the flight deck. As the bow rose, a rolling mass of green water would cascade down the flight deck. As the wave passed and the stern of the ship sank into the trough, all this water would pour of the after end of the flight deck in a huge waterfall which from a distance looked like Niagara Falls. The smaller ships, cruisers and destroyers were hidden most of the time in clouds of spray. The whole fleet was steaming along at about 10 knots, which was quite fast in such a heavy sea. At least the conditions made it difficult for U-boats to operate, and we never saw signs of any during the whole operation.

On signalling what we thought to be the American Admiral's flagship, we found that they had lost several men overboard on the way over in the rough weather – including the Admiral in command of the fleet. We could not help wondering what the Americans were feeling about their first foray into European waters.

In the process of meeting and then taking up position ahead of the fleet to escort it the two or three hundred miles to Scapa, we had some excellent views of the ships. Every vantage point on our ship was crowded with crew members armed with cameras. Conditions for photography were ideal, with the bright sun illuminating the deep blue colour of the sea and brilliant white of the breaking wave tops and spray. I eventually ended up with a dozen or so excellent photographs, all of which unfortunately were lost when the ship was subsequently lost in action. It seems, however, that someone on board managed to get his photographs back home. Many months later, after returning home as a survivor of the sinking, I bought a copy of *Picture Post* (a news magazine of photographs) and the whole paper was taken up with pictures of the arrival of the American Fleet. The same photographs as I had taken but had lost.

Rumours, or 'buzzes' as they were called, were always rife on board. After some months of patrol work and a couple of convoys to Murmansk and Archangel in North Russia, a persistent buzz circulated that we were going to dock for a refit. This could only happen by our returning to a U.K. port, and there was great excitement at the thought of such a prospect and the possibility of some home leave, or at least getting ashore where there were some reasonable facilities. Shore leave since I joined the ship had consisted of the occasional evening ashore at Scapa or Valfjord in Iceland. Facilities at these bases were minimal and the weather usually so inhospitable that we often did not bother going ashore, preferring the relative comfort of our shipboard recreation room and library, and perhaps a cinema show put on in one of the aircraft hangars.

The refit buzz was finally confirmed when the Captain informed us that our next trip would be to North Shields on the river Tyne, where a full refit was to take place over a number of months. Everyone on board would get three weeks' leave. Great jubilation and cheers all round!

It is difficult to describe the feeling which this news engendered. A sort of relief. Being at sea in a war zone brings an odd sort of sensation. You are not actually in action, but you never know when action might start. It usually starts without warning, and literally 'with a bang'. For days and weeks on end nothing happens; it is depressingly boring; plodding along at five or six knots on a ship that can do 30 knots, patrolling or escorting a convoy. Someone once described Russian convoy duty as entailing 'long periods of sheer boredom punctuated by short periods of intense activity', and they were right. There is a sense of constant threat; especially when being shadowed by enemy long-range aircraft which circle round, carefully keeping just out of range of our guns, but all the while reporting our position to their base and any U-boats in the area. There was a story going around about these shadowing aircraft. A convoy leaving Iceland had, as usual, quickly been spotted by a long-range Focke-Wulf Condor, which circled the convoy day after day, just out of range. The story went that the escorting cruiser, getting fed up with the aircraft's monotonous circling, signalled to it: 'You're making us dizzy, can't you go round in the opposite direction?', to which the reply came: 'Anything to oblige an Englishman,' followed by the plane altering to a reciprocal course.

The news that we were returning to the U.K. lifted this threat, and suddenly it felt as though a weight had been lifted off us. Although we still had to get down the North Sea to the Tyne, this seemed like a 'cake-walk' compared with operating in northern waters. It was therefore with some jubilation that we left Scapa one day and turned south instead of the usual north. It was Spring, early March, and we were looking forward to seeing green fields when we made our landfall, instead of the snow-covered landscape which greeted us when arriving in Russia. Unknown to us, the U.K. was having a late winter, and we were somewhat disgusted when the northeast coast of England hove in sight and we found it covered in snow. We arrived in South Shields in blizzard conditions. However, the cold was nothing like as intense as in the Arctic, and the snow disappeared after a couple of days.

We were in the dry dock in South Shields for a couple of months and by the time we left we were fed up to the teeth with it. The ship, which was our home, was not ours while it was in dock. There were 'dockies' (dockyard workers) all over the place, working at various jobs in every conceivable corner of the ship. Because we were in a dry dock, we had to go ashore to wash and bathe and use toilets, and all the rubbish which usually went down a chute over the ship's side had to be carted ashore. Our normal shipboard life and routine went completely by the board. Granted, we had shore leave every evening, and there were more 'attractions' in South Shields than in Scapa Flow or Iceland, but it was not much of a 'home' to come back to after being ashore. The ship's company went on 'long' leave in two watches. This meant that half the crew went off on home leave when we arrived in dock, and when they returned after three weeks, the other half took off. I was lucky and was in the first half to go, so a couple of days after arriving in England I was at home in Bangor very quickly, getting used again to all the luxuries of home life.

Jottings of a Young Sailor

On returning from leave, my first sight of the ship on entering the docks was of it resplendent in brand new camouflage paint. All sorts of light greys and greens and blues. I went on board to find all sorts of 'buzzes' and rumours about us going south into the sun. There was talk of Freetown in Africa and all sorts of other exotic places.

When a ship refits, apart from repairing and refitting the ship itself, crew changes also take place for a variety of reasons. People get promoted and go off to another ship; some go off on training courses. If there are to be any personnel changes it usually happens when the ship is refitting. We C.W. candidates who had done our sea time were hoping for the next stage in our officer training programme. This was an interview at a selection board comprising the Captain of our ship and other senior officers. Those who passed this board would leave the ship and go on to one of the officer training schools for further training. Alas, it did not happen. No replacements for us arrived, so we had to accept the fact that we were going to spend some more time at sea before going ashore to continue our training. The trouble was, we knew that once at sea in a newly refitted ship, it was unlikely we would get off it for some time to come. We would be on active service and would only be released if replacements arrived. Our only hope was that the shortage of officers would persuade the powers that be to get replacements for us sooner rather than later. In the event, replacements never arrived and the only way we got off the ship was when it was sunk!

Because of the departure and arrival of personnel on the mess decks, and my consequent elevation in the hierarchical structure, I was now able to sling my hammock actually in my own mess deck, and now also had the luxury of my own personal locker in the mess. I had arrived at last! This newly found status also meant that when off duty at sea I could also 'get my head down', or sleep, in the mess in any available space. This was usually on top of the mess table or on form seats alongside it, or on top of the lockers. Anywhere would do so long as it was up off the deck which, at sea, usually had two or three inches of water swilling back and forth as the ship rolled in the swell. The lockers were about two-foot-six in height and were stacked in batches of two on top of each other around the mess. They were made of aluminium and in true Naval fashion were polished until they shone like mirrors.

On one occasion I was lying asleep on top of these lockers while off duty. The locker I was lying on was immediately opposite the mess table (lower down), which was similarly occupied by two of my messmates, sleeping end to end. As sometimes happened at sea, the intercom came to life with an announcement from the bridge that the ship would shortly alter course and may roll heavily. We did not always take a great deal of notice of this announcement, and on this occasion no one did. Shortly afterwards, the ship did indeed roll – so heavily that I suddenly slid off the top of the lockers I was lying on and landed, hammock, bedclothes and all, on top of the two sailors sleeping on the mess table. The table collapsed, knocking over the adjoining forms, complete with their own recumbent and snoring sailors. This resulted in a sort of soup comprising half a dozen irate sailors, broken table and forms, hammocks, bedclothes, sea boots and other miscellaneous items all sliding backwards and forwards across the mess deck in three or four inches of water as the ship rolled violently from side to side. All of a sudden the peaceful silence of the sleeping mess deck was broken by a tirade of colourful language, calling into question the parentage of all and sundry and me in particular, since I was the unfortunate one who happened to land on top of everyone else. The Officer of the watch on the bridge also came in for his share of abuse for not keeping the ship on an even keel.

Jottings of a Young Sailor

The refit eventually ended; with mixed feelings. On the one hand we were glad to get our ship (home) back out of the hands of the dockyard maties who had ruled our world for the last weeks. On the other hand, we wondered what awaited us when we got back to sea on active service. The war at sea was hotting up and we knew that no matter what part of the world we went to, there would be no 'easy tickets'. Nevertheless, when the day came for us to leave Tyneside there was a certain eagerness to get back again, doing what we had been trained for. We were looking forward, after leaving harbour, to the Captain's announcement on the intercom as to what our next assignment would be. We were half hoping that we would proceed to warmer climes; and when the expected announcement came we were somewhat disappointed to hear that we were returning to Scapa Flow to await orders. This seemed to point towards more patrolling and convoy duty in Northern waters.

It was now April 1942. Assembled at Reykjavik, in the southeast corner of Iceland, was the biggest convoy yet marshalled to attempt the hazardous voyage to Murmansk. This was convoy PQ14 and bore the codeword 'Credence'. Convoys to north Russia were, at this time, numbered with the prefix letters PQ, and those returning QP. The convoy's cruiser escort was H.M.S. *Edinburgh*.

Before leaving Scapa Flow for Iceland, we took on board a rather unusual cargo consisting of a number of large steel plates. These were urgently needed to repair the cruiser *Trinidad*, now lying in dry dock in the Kola inlet near Murmansk.

The torpedoing of the *Trinidad* was in itself one of the most extraordinary events of the war. While escorting PQ13 to Murmansk, *Trinidad* engaged three German destroyers, destroying one and badly damaging another. In the engagement *Trinidad* fired a torpedo to finish off the damaged enemy ship. The torpedo missed its target, circled round and exploded in

Trinidad's own port side, killing 32 men and causing a severe list. With skilled seamanship, *Trinidad* limped back to Rosta in the Kola inlet. The Russians were quite prepared to supply the labour to effect repairs, but could not supply the steel plates necessary to patch the 60ft by 20ft hole in the cruiser's side. The only plates available were somewhere in the Rosta dockyard, buried under tons of snow!

PQ14 comprised 23 merchantmen carrying tanks, planes, ammunition and trucks. The ships sailed on Wednesday 8th April 1942, accompanied by eight small escorts of anti-submarine trawlers and armed minesweepers. They made their way along the north coast of Iceland towards a rendezvous with *Edinburgh* off the north-eastern coast of Iceland. It was not long before things began to go wrong. The edge of the polar ice shelf was considerably further south than had been expected. By Sunday morning the convoy and its escorts ran into thick drifting ice. In the meantime *Edinburgh*, with Rear Admiral Sir Stuart Bonham Carter KCB, CB, CVO, DSO commanding the 18th cruiser squadron on board, and with her own escorts – the destroyers *Forrester* and *Foresight* – left Scapa Flow for the rendezvous. Thick fog was soon encountered, but with the escorts keeping station by radar, *Edinburgh* proceeded on without altering course or speed. Disturbing signals were then received from the convoy escorts further north. Several of the escort ships had sustained damage in the ice. Three of the anti-submarine trawlers were so badly damaged they had to return to Iceland, as did some of the merchant ships. In the dense fog, the merchantmen also found themselves in the ice field. The heavily loaded vessels found themselves surrounded by and colliding with large solid tables of ice. In some cases, ships were cannoning into a compact wall of the icefield itself. It would have been bad enough in good visibility, but in blanket fog it became a nightmare. Once in, they had to get out – but which way was out? Hulls got buckled, plates ruptured, causing flooding, stems were crushed and propeller blades dismembered. It was a bad beginning to a voyage that promised so much.

When the fog cleared and *Edinburgh* joined the convoy, only eight merchant ships were present, with an impressive escort of six destroyers, four corvettes, four minesweepers and two trawlers. By Tuesday 14th, the convoy was about a third of the way to Russia and had not yet been detected, thanks mainly to the fog. The following morning two of the destroyers picked up U-boat contacts and raced off, dropping patterns of depth charges without any apparent result other than chasing the U-boats out of the area. That evening we spotted a German reconnaissance plane circling the convoy well out of range, and we knew our position was now known to the German naval bases in Norway and also any U-boats in the area. By Thursday, the convoy was just south of Bear Island, a remote spot nearly 75 degrees north at the edge of the ice barrier. This was where convoys had to run the gauntlet between the ice barrier immediately north of them and the German planes, submarines and destroyers coming out of their Norwegian bases not far to the south.

The *Edinburgh*'s function was to defend the convoy against surface or air attack; the destroyers and other small warships being the main defence against U-boats. When two torpedo tracks were seen crossing our bows, the Admiral ordered the ship to speed westwards and take up position a mile or so astern of the convoy. Numerous U-boat contacts were picked up and U-boats spotted on the surface ahead of the convoy. The close escort destroyers were kept busy, weaving around dropping patterns of depth charges and engaging with gunfire any submarine sighted on the surface. Meanwhile, the convoy plodded along at eight knots in four columns of three ships each, with *Empire Howard* in the forward column. Several U-boats were sighted on the surface and were immediately pursued by a number of the close escort ships. It was thought afterwards that this was a deliberate ploy by the U-boats to lure the escorts away from the convoy, because another U-boat managed to slip undetected inside the escort screen and fired a salvo of three torpedoes at the *Empire Howard*. No one saw the tracks, and there was a blinding flash as the first torpedo plunged into the starboard side, exploding in the boiler room; a few seconds later the second smashed its way into the engine room; then the third struck between No 4 and 5 holds and the magazine exploded in a mighty eruption of flame, smoke and steam. No ship could stand such an onslaught. Within half a minute the water was up to the bridge ladders. A minute after the first torpedo had struck, the ship was gone, leaving only some debris, life rafts and some of her crew struggling in the water, which was well below freezing point.

There then followed an episode which illustrates the horrors of the war at sea.

When *Empire Howard* was hit, two anti-submarine trawlers astern of the convoy raced towards the stricken vessel, their tasks twofold; to attack the U-boat with depth charges and to rescue survivors. The *Northern Wave* was first to arrive and the young captain, an R.N.R. Lieutenant, was faced with an agonising decision. Thrashing about in the sea in the trawlers' path, in an area of black oil and debris, were 38 men, waving, screaming and pleading to be saved. The U-boat which had attacked the convoy was in the area immediately below them. If the captain attacked the submarine with depth charges, the concussion effect would kill many of those in the water. If he ignored the submarine and saved those in the water, the U-boat would escape and kill and maim ten times as many. The inevitable decision was to attack, and ten depth charges, set at differing depths, were catapulted from the thrower. Only those some distance from the explosions survived the shock waves. The remainder died instantly from broken necks or internal injuries. As *Northern Wave* approached, it was seen there were many still in life jackets who neither waved nor shouted but gazed at them with sightless eyes, bobbing up and down in the Arctic swell. Out of *Empire Howard's* crew of 54, only 18 were rescued and of these, nine died aboard the trawlers.

Penetration of the destroyer screen and the subsequent sinking of *Empire Howard* was of grave concern to the Admiral. We were only half way through the 2,000 mile voyage and entering the most dangerous stretch, between Bear Island and Murmansk. He became even more concerned when a signal from Admiralty informed him that enemy destroyers were leaving their base in north Norway with the intention of attacking the convoy. To offset this threat, *Edinburgh* now took up a position ten miles ahead of the convoy and a little to the south.

The weather, which had been such a hindrance at the start of the voyage, now came to the convoy's aid. The German flotilla, much further south, had run into a force nine gale and heavy snow. The sea washing over their decks froze and covered the ships with a thick coating of ice. Binoculars, telescopes, and gun sights became useless. The guns froze solid and could not be fired. The group commanding officer ordered his ships to return to base. Admiral Bonham Carter was unaware of this withdrawal, but it was at this point that we were again blessed with a turn in the weather, in the form of thick fog which hid the convoy, its escorts and *Edinburgh* from detection. The fog could not have come at a more fortunate time, because about 14 enemy planes arrived and we would most certainly have been dive-bombed if they had found us. The planes stayed for half an hour while we played a dangerous game of hide and seek in the fog. They criss-crossed and circled overhead, looking for a gap. As the evening of the 18th wore on, the fog thickened and the aircraft eventually abandoned their search for us and departed.

The following day, the fog had dispersed and a force nine gale was blowing. At this point, *Edinburgh*, accompanied by the destroyers *Foresight* and *Forrester*, left the convoy and arrived in the Kola inlet, leading to Murmansk, at 11 p.m. on Saturday 19th April. As we made our way upstream, the temperature was 10 degrees below zero, and the intermittent sleet turned to snow, the flakes heaping where they fell. The snow fluttered silently down to pile up against the forward gun turrets and superstructure, and the masts and yardarms became white woolly trees. The snow brought an unnatural hush to the activities of the fo'c'sle hands as they padded their way across the snow-covered deck. Ice floes floating down river were pushed aside as we steamed slowly up river. We anchored at Vaenga, a few miles north of Murmansk, where we hoped to escape the worst of the Murmansk air raids from the German airfields behind the Finnish front line, about 20 miles to the west. At this time of year there is 24 hours of daylight, so that the air alarms were a constant irritant and the 4-inch anti-aircraft guns were manned continually. One of the biggest frights of my life happened one day when I happened to wander out on to the 4-inch gun deck just at the time when, unknown by me, a German plane approached. Without warning, the starboard battery of four twin 4-inch guns opened up right beside me with such an enormous bang it nearly split my eardrums – besides nearly making me jump over the side with fright. It was difficult at times to get any sleep, because the 4-inch batteries would open up every time a German plane came anywhere near us, and even down below decks the unexpected blasting off of the 4-inch guns made a lot of noise and was quite a shock.

It was now late April, a time of continuous daylight in these latitudes, and the nine days we remained at Vianga seemed to pass relatively quickly. This was probably because there was continuous activity. In addition to the constant air raids, injured survivors of previous convoys were brought aboard for medical treatment by our doctors. Medical facilities at Murmansk were practically non-existent at the time. There was loading and unloading. The cruiser *Trinidad*, lying damaged in dry dock at Rosta further up the river with a gaping hole in her side, claimed first priority. Not only did she urgently need the steel plates we had brought from the U.K., but she was also desperately short of stores following her enforced stay in north Russia, with no means of obtaining supplies of food and warm clothing. The steel plates were craned into two barges secured alongside and taken up river to *Trinidad*. One of our boats was loaded with fresh food, potatoes and a supply of warm clothing. Then there was the loading of the 'ammunition', which turned out not to be ammunition at all.

Two days before the end of our stay at Vaenga there was a commotion at midnight, although it was still quite light at the time with the midnight sun. Two barges had secured alongside on the starboard side, and at vantage points on the barges were Russian soldiers with 'Tommy' guns held at the ready. On our own ship, stationed at regular intervals from the deck and up ladders to the flight deck, our own Royal Marines were keeping guard. As we watched, the tarpaulins covering the barge's cargo were drawn back to reveal a load of ammunition boxes. But why such security for what seemed like a normal cargo to be loading onto a warship? It was not long before the truth was out. The boxes contained not ammunition but gold bullion; over five tons of it to be shipped to the U.K. in part payment for the war materials and equipment being sent to Russia by Britain and America. (At the time, the gold would have been worth something in the order of £5 million, but the gold recovered in a subsequent salvage operation in 1981 was valued at £45 million, and another £3 million was not recovered.) The boxes, with rope handles, were extremely heavy, each needing two men to lift.

Norman Sparksman

In the dull grey daylight of the Arctic midnight, we hauled the boxes all the way up to the flight deck and then lowered them down a shaft by ropes to the bomb room at the bottom of the ship, three decks below. The odd thing was that the whole time the gold was being loaded there was a feeling of uneasiness. Sailors are superstitious people and the apprehensiveness increased when half way through the operation sleet started falling and made the heavy red stencilling on the boxes run in a trail of scarlet drips on the snow-covered deck. 'Russian gold dripping with blood,' someone commented. Was this a bad omen?

Chapter 3

Convoy QP11

The day before we left the Kola inlet, the Captain announced some details of the convoy we were to escort back to Iceland. The convoy would consist of 13 merchant ships. Seven were British, five were American and there was one Russian ship. The convoy sailed on Tuesday 28th April 1942, with *Edinburgh* and a destroyer escort close astern. The departure was watched by the Germans, who had occupied a distant cape to the west, and was reported to German Naval Command Norway. Thus the wheels were set in motion to attack and destroy the westward bound convoy.

Three heavily armed destroyers left the German naval port of Kirkenes in north Norway with orders to attack convoy

QP11. In addition, instructions were sent to seven U-boats in the northern area to close in on the convoy in support of the German surface vessels.

The convoy's close escort of destroyers and corvettes was quite adequate to deal with U-boat attacks, but none of them were sufficiently armed to repulse successfully a heavy air attack; neither were they capable of engaging the large, heavily armed Narvik class destroyers on anything like equal terms. However, *Edinburgh* was certainly expected to match any destroyer attack which might be mounted.

With *Edinburgh* steaming along patiently astern of the six-knot convoy, the thin strip of coastline soon disappeared as the ships headed due north towards the edge of the ice barrier before turning westwards toward home. It was not long before the northeast wind brought the usual snow storms and rough sea. Conditions made life difficult for the empty merchant ships riding high in the sea with propellers half out of the water, wallowing and rolling in the rough sea. It was no less difficult for the close escort vessels steaming up through the line of ships, shepherding strays into line and persuading laggards to increase speed to keep up into station.

By early morning on 29th April, barely 24 hours after sailing, the enemy found the convoy. A Junkers Ju 88 patrol plane arrived and commenced the customary circling, being very careful to stay just out of range of our guns whilst transmitting to base details of the convoy's position, speed, direction etc. To be spotted so early in the voyage did not bode well for the convoy.

Admiral Schmundt at the German naval base in Norway was in command of the German forces opposing the convoy, and was immensely satisfied with the reports coming in so soon after the convoy's departure. He knew that the convoy presently proceeding north would soon have to turn west to avoid the ice barrier, and all he need do was to put his forces in place ahead

Jottings of a Young Sailor

of the convoy and wait for it to arrive. He ordered his destroyer group, consisting of the *Hermann Shoemann, Z24* and *Z25*, to be ready to put to sea and his U-boats to take up station ahead of the estimated course of the convoy. Also he alerted a new force of torpedo-carrying aircraft.

The convoy was soon engaged in frequently altering its course to avoid ice fields, and the following morning frequent sightings of U-boats made further course alterations necessary, with the close escort of destroyers speeding around dropping depth charges. With the constant presence of U-boats, it was no place for a large cruiser to be proceeding along at the six-knot speed of the convoy, and *Edinburgh* left the rear of the convoy and took up station about 20 miles ahead of the leading ships, zigzagging all the while to avoid torpedo attack.

Lieutenant Max Teichert, in command of U 456, was returning to base to replenish supplies after a patrol in the Barents Sea when he was ordered to take up position ahead of convoy QP11. He rose to periscope depth close ahead of the convoy and saw, not the numerous masts of merchant ships he expected, but a large unaccompanied cruiser, the *Edinburgh*. Not an escort vessel in sight. Not an opportunity to be missed. He only had two torpedoes left and carefully planned his attack, taking into account the cruiser's zigzagging course, speed and range. He gave the order 'fire one' and a few seconds later, 'fire two'. The vibration of the torpedoes leaving the tubes echoed through the submarine as the deadly warheads sped towards their unsuspecting target.

On board *Edinburgh*, the ship's company were closed up at 'Action Stations' because of the known presence of U-boats and because we knew that the enemy knew of our position. My action station was on a piece of equipment called the deflection screen in the after H.A.T.S. (high angle transmitting station). There were two of these stations, one forward and one aft. They consisted of a room about 20 feet square filled with all the latest equipment to aid the accurate sighting and firing of the ship's secondary armament of sixteen 4-inch guns. The rooms were situated in the bottom of the ship underneath a 4-inch thick armour-plated deck. There was only one way into and out of these rooms and that was through a hatchway with a 4-inch steel hatch so heavy it needed a chain pulley to open or close it. At Action Stations the hatch was closed and sealed from the outside so that no one inside could get out until someone outside opened it. Each H.A.T.S. was manned by about 10 men who operated the various instruments attached to the 'Table' in the centre of the room.

I was at my station when the first torpedo struck amidships on the starboard side. There was a muffled bump, as if the ship had hit something solid, and a slight roll as she leaned over and then righted again. I have a distinct recollection of hearing one of the more experienced sailors muttering, 'That was a —in' tin fish!' I didn't know it at the time, but the torpedo left a hole in the ship's side large enough to drive a double decker bus through. It went through the 4-inch thick armour plating like a hot knife through butter.

A few seconds later, the second torpedo struck with much more dramatic effect. It landed in the compartment next to the one we were in. An enormous bang, with much rattling and scraping of metal, and all the lights went out, leaving us in complete darkness. The ship gave such a heave, we all lost our footing and fell down on the deck. Much too close for comfort! The darkness we had been plunged into took on a sort of blue hue, owing to the colourful language emanating from the heap of bodies, arms and legs rolling around on the deck. One of the pieces of equipment in the H.A.T.S. was a bicycle frame bolted to the deck with a belt drive from the back wheel to a dynamo on the deck. This was intended to provide emergency lighting in the event of a

Jottings of a Young Sailor

power failure. I remember jumping on to this bicycle, pedalling furiously and being very thankful when the pitch blackness was broken by a glimmer from the emergency lighting. At least we could now see what was going on in the room.

My station in the H.A.T.S involved, amongst other things, wearing a headset for communication with the director tower, from where the guns were controlled, and also the bridge. I remember calling the bridge to test communications and was glad to find the line working. I enquired what was going on and was curtly told not to be asking silly questions as they were rather busy up there just then. By now, the rest of the crew in the room had picked themselves up from the deck and were busily engaged in testing the various instruments on the 'table' which they were responsible for operating.

Unknown to us, the damage-control parties had been hard at work since the first 'hit' and it was not long before full power was restored. This came as something of a relief, as we were getting rather tired of pedalling the 'bike' to keep a glimmer of light and power going. Rather surprisingly we found that all of our instruments were operating satisfactorily, and we were able to report to the bridge that our station was fully operational. This time the bridge were a little more forthcoming and informed us we had been hit by two torpedoes, one amidships and one right aft (as if we didn't already know). We were also informed that there was a suspected fire in the after 6-inch magazine. This did little to raise our spirits, since this magazine was immediately below and next door to us. However, not long afterwards the bridge advised that the magazine had been flooded and the danger averted. The even more welcome news was that since the immediate threat to the ship was from submarines, the secondary armament would not be immediately required and the after H.A.T.S could be evacuated. Someone was being dispatched to open the armour-plated hatch which was sealing us in.

Convoy QP11 to Iceland

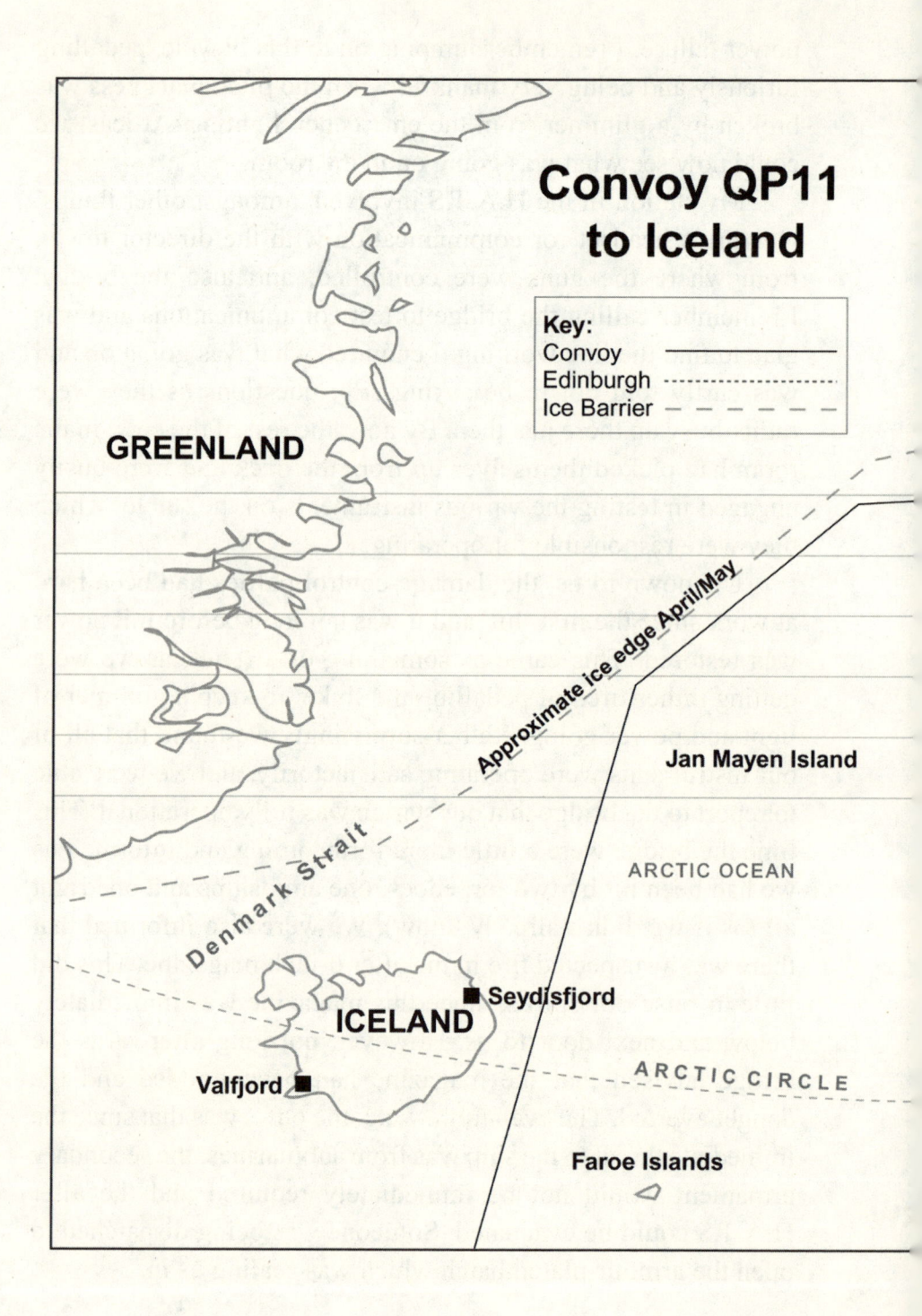

Key:
Convoy ———
Edinburgh ·············
Ice Barrier — — —

GREENLAND

Approximate ice edge April/May

Jan Mayen Island

Denmark Strait

ARCTIC OCEAN

ICELAND
Seydisfjord
Valfjord

ARCTIC CIRCLE

Faroe Islands

Jottings of a Young Sailor

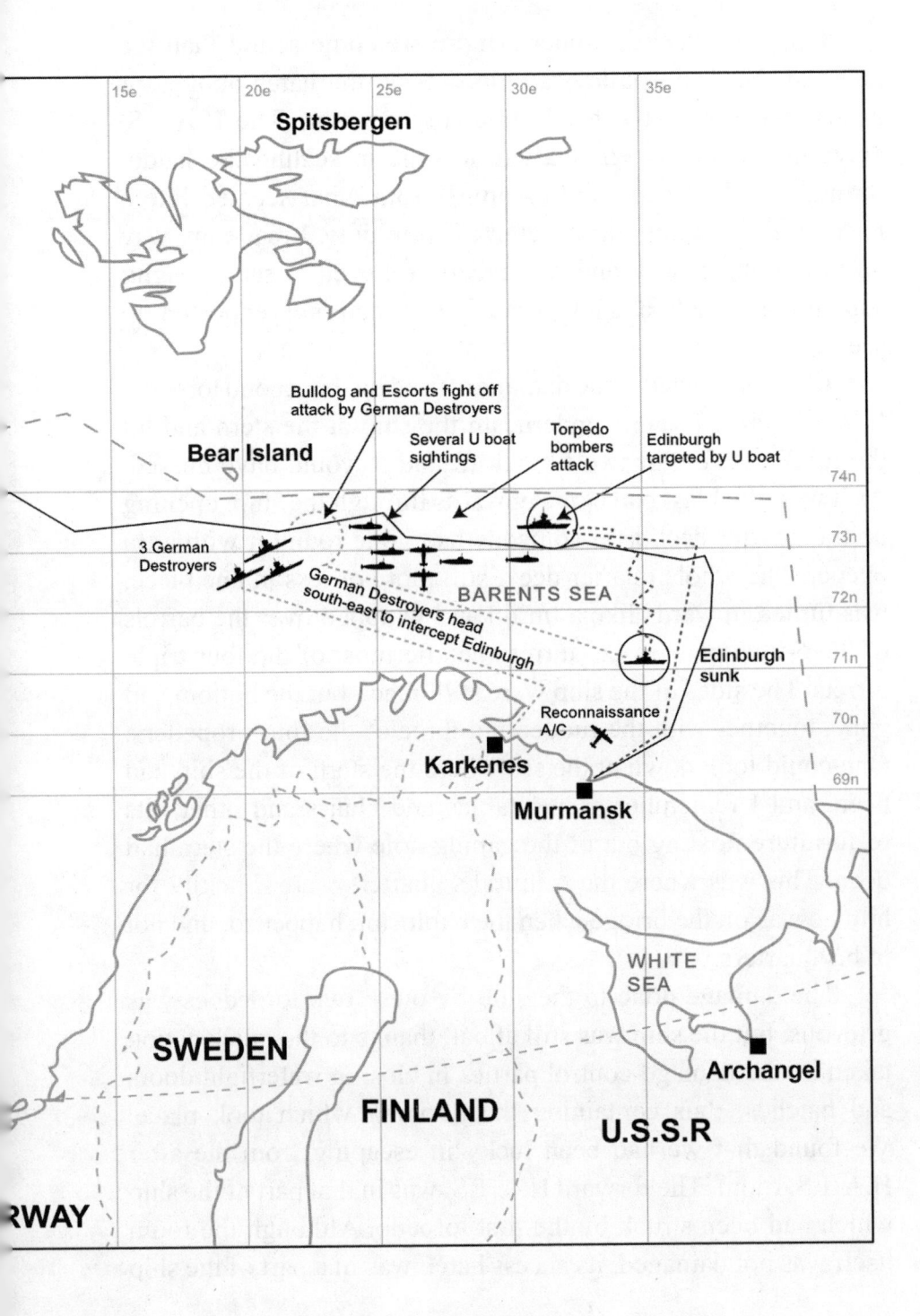

I cannot ever remember a more welcome sound than the noise of the chain pulley rattling outside the hatch above our heads, and seeing the hatch gradually opening. The H.A.T.S. crew, including myself, wasted no time in scaling the ladder through the hatchway and escaping from what seemed like a rat trap. Being temporarily relieved from duty, I made my way up to the upper deck and was greatly relieved to see daylight; something which a short time ago I had not expected to see again.

I was astounded at the damage caused by the second torpedo. It had apparently gone underneath the ship at the stern and hit the rudder. A foot or two further aft and it would have missed. As it was, the blast had come upwards through the ship, opening up the quarter-deck as if someone had gone round it with a tin opener. The whole quarter-deck, still more or less in one piece, was turned upwards like a tin lid and wrapped over the barrels of the 6-inch guns in 'Y' turret, the aftermost of the four triple turrets. The sides of the ship were still intact, but the bottom had gone, together with the rudder and three of the four propellers. One could look down at the sea where the stern of the ship had been, and I remember seeing tables and chairs and other bits of furniture floating out of the gaping hole where the stern had been. This was where the Admiral's quarters were. Luckily for him he was on the bridge when the explosion happened, and not in his quarters.

The damage done to the ship by these two torpedoes was grievous, but the ship was still afloat, thanks to the quick action taken by the damage-control parties in closing watertight doors and hatches, thus containing the flooding which took place. We found that we had been lucky in escaping from the after H.A.T.S. room. The forward H.A.T.S. was in that part of the ship which had been struck by the first torpedo. Although the room itself was not damaged, its access hatch was in a part of the ship which had been flooded. Although the crew were unharmed by the explosion, there was no way they could get out. We never saw them again.

In the meantime, the convoy, now some miles to the north, was steaming steadily westwards with its close escort of destroyers and corvettes. A signal was sent to the leading destroyer, *Bulldog*, reporting that *Edinburgh* had been torpedoed and requesting assistance. However, the convoy's escort was having its own problems. U-boats had been sighted ahead and astern of the convoy, and the escorts were speeding around dropping depth charges in an attempt to ward off an attack. Despite the fact that he was loath to deplete his own force, the commander of the escorts dispatched the British destroyers *Foresight* and *Forrester* and two Russian destroyers to investigate.

When the destroyers reached the *Edinburgh*, they found her in a sorry state. The explosion had left a gaping hole 50 feet wide in her starboard side, through which hundreds of tons of water was surging in and out and pressurising bulkheads weakened by the blast. Aft, the wrecked stern and propeller shafts made the ship completely unmanageable. The Kola inlet was 250 miles away but an attempt had to be made to get a tow under way. A formidable piece of seamanship. With *Foresight* and the two Russian destroyers acting as a screen against further attack, *Forrester* managed to pass a line to *Edinburgh*'s fo'c'sle. Conditions were grim. The sub-zero temperature and cold wind had turned the deck into a sheet of ice, making it nearly impossible to maintain a foothold as the ship rose and fell in the swell. The heavy wire hawsers used for the tow were cumbersome and almost unmanageable because of icing. Eventually a wire was secured and *Forrester* took the strain and started to tow. With no means of steering, it was a clumsy and awkward tow, yawing wildly from side to side as the wind-swept rollers first lifted the bow high in the air and then dropped it with a crash into the next trough. It was not long before the intermittent jerking strain on the tow wire proved too much and the wire snapped with the sound of a rifle shot. Four more unsuccessful attempts were made before towing from the bow was abandoned.

Meanwhile, with the aid of acetylene cutters, some of the wreckage at the stern had been released. It fell away, and the ship was able to make some headway under its own power and its single propeller; but with no rudder or means of steering, it was impossible to keep a steady course. It was decided to pass a line to *Forrester* from aft in an effort to control the stern action. Again, this was no mean feat of seamanship. I well remember being one of the fo'c'sle party detailed to manhandle a length of our anchor cable from the fo'c'sle, where it was normally stored, to the quarterdeck at the other end of the ship, where it was to be secured to act as a spring on the end of the tow wire which was to be passed to *Forrester*. Every link on this cable, which in total weighed several tons, had a film of ice coating it, so that it was very difficult to hold. In addition, the ice-covered decks were like skating rinks, rising and falling and twisting on the ocean swell. The cable had to be moved – by hand – the length of the ship, then down ladders to the level of the quarterdeck, which was two decks below the fo'c'sle deck.

We had not had much sleep or food during the last 24 hours and were tired and cold, but we set to with a will because we all realised that the very survival of the ship might depend on our efforts. With some difficulty we eventually managed to drag the cable foot by foot down to the quarterdeck. At this point someone sighted a U-boat on the surface barely three miles away, and *Forrester* dashed off to attack. We did not know it at the time, but the U-boat was the one which had torpedoed us with its last torpedoes. Not having anything to finish us off with, he was shadowing us and reporting our position back to his base. When *Forrester* approached, he crash-dived deep and waited silently. Unfortunately, *Forrester* had an engine room problem which inhibited the attack and enabled the U-boat to escape with only a smashed periscope. However, this did mean she could not 'see' without surfacing, a risk her commander was not willing to take.

While *Forrester* was off chasing the submarine, *Foresight* came in and managed to get a line on to our stern. We steamed slowly forward, towing *Foresight*, which acted as a kind of rudder to keep us on course. This manoeuvre proved reasonably successful, and with *Forrester* and two Russian destroyers which had now arrived on the scene accompanying us, we moved at about three knots southwards towards the Kola Inlet during the night and early hours of 1st May. At about six o'clock in the morning, the Russian destroyers indicated that they were running short of oil and would have to return to Murmansk to refuel. This was a setback, because *Foresight* then had to cast off to join *Forrester* in providing an anti-submarine screen around us, since it was known there were U-boats in the vicinity.

With no means of steering, *Edinburgh* again started her wild gyrations, at times moving in a complete circle, and progress towards the safety of Murmansk slowed to two knots. Meanwhile, numerous signals were coming in, raising and then dashing our hopes as they arrived: A Russian tug was on its way in company of the British minesweepers *Harrier*, *Niger*, *Hussar* and *Gossamer* ... Many enemy submarines were taking up position between *Edinburgh* and the Kola Inlet ... Enemy destroyers were at sea and heading for *Edinburgh* ... The German pocket battleship *Admiral Scheer* (sister ship of the notorious *Graf Spee* which had been scuttled at Montevideo early in the war) had left Trondheim and was loose in the Arctic. If she found us, the end would be swift and certain.

Meanwhile, convoy QP11 was steaming slowly along the edge of the ice cap, some 200 miles to the northwest, in company of the escorts led by *Bulldog*. As usual, the convoy was being shadowed by German long-range Focke Wulf Condor planes, so that its exact location at any time was known by the enemy. It was not long before a group of Heinkel He 111 long-range bombers appeared, each carrying two torpedoes. The defensive fire from the convoy escort was so effective that the bombers were not able to concentrate sufficiently, and their torpedoes were dropped inaccurately, speeding off and disappearing harmlessly amongst the ice floes.

Because *Edinburgh* was now crippled and disabled, she could no longer carry out her function of protecting the convoy from attack by heavy enemy surface forces. The convoy to the northwest was therefore now virtually defenceless against such attack. The German naval command in Norway knew this, and lost no time dispatching a flotilla of three heavy destroyers, *Z24*, *Z25* and *Hermann Schoemann*. These were modern ships, and would outgun any of our ships except *Edinburgh* – but she was now crippled and unmanoeuvrable, although she did have one 6-inch gun turret of three guns still capable of firing under local control. The three German destroyers had been dispatched from Norway with orders to find convoy QP11, dispose of the lesser-gunned escort then pick off the merchant ships one by one. Having done this, they would then proceed to *Edinburgh*, which was being trailed by a U-boat, and finish her off. On paper this seemed a relatively easy task for these heavily armed warships. In the event, things did not work out quite like that.

The German destroyers found the convoy around midday on 1st May in poor visibility with constant snow showers. They immediately prepared their attack but were beaten off by the spirited defence of the convoy escort. In the ensuing battle they attacked six times, but despite their superior firepower were unable to break through the defence to attack the convoy, which in the meantime had entered the ice field in an endeavour to escape the torpedoes which were coming towards them from both enemy destroyers and submarines. One of these stray torpedoes struck the Russian freighter with a massive explosion. The ship came to a halt, settled by the bows with her screws high in the water, plunged down and was gone.

By six o'clock in the evening, the German destroyers had used up two-thirds of their ammunition. They abandoned the engagement with the convoy and its escorts and headed for the crippled *Edinburgh*, 200 miles to the southeast. The somewhat bruised escort rounded up the convoy and headed to the west and home.

Meanwhile, *Edinburgh*, crawling along at two knots, had made little progress towards the Kola inlet 200 miles away. Only by using the engines could she be prevented from going around in circles. At least we were moving and not presenting a 'sitting duck' to the waiting U-boats, whose presence triggered off constant alarms and kept us at action stations most of the time. We were beginning to feel the effects of lack of sleep and proper food.

At about 1800 hours on 1st May, lookouts spotted a small ship approaching from the southeast. Since my normal action station in the H.A.T.S. had been evacuated, I had taken up a new station with one of the 4-inch gun crews. It happened to be one of these gunners who had spotted the small ship. The gun I was on was quickly loaded and trained on the approaching ship, ready to fire. On closer approach it was found that the ship was a small Russian tug sent out to tow us to Murmansk, and preparations immediately started to secure a line to our bows. Around midnight, with the Arctic sun still not below the horizon, the four minesweepers *Hussar*, *Harrier*, *Gossamer* and *Niger* arrived. These were each armed with two 4-inch guns. Our hopes rose when this little flotilla gathered around us, but were soon dashed again when it was found that the Russian tug did not have sufficient power to tow *Edinburgh* on her own. We managed to secure another line forward to *Gossamer*, who, with the tug, started to move us ahead but still very slowly. So, with *Foresight* and *Forrester* on each beam and *Harrier*, *Niger* and *Hussar* astern, we were under way again and heading for Murmansk, towed by *Gossamer* and the Russian tug at about three knots.

Meanwhile, the three German destroyers were racing towards *Edinburgh* from the northwest at 35 knots. They found the oil slick we were trailing for miles behind, and in poor visibility, with fog and intermittent snow showers, planned their torpedo attack. A classic attack; line ahead until within range, then turn abreast about a mile apart and fire all torpedoes at the same time. It was improbable that, with her lack of manoeuvrability, *Edinburgh* would be able to escape such a concentration of cross fire.

The first we knew of the enemy's close approach was when we heard gunfire. *Hussar* behind us saw the German destroyers looming out of the mist and immediately opened fire with her two 4-inch guns. Despite a spirited resistance, she was outgunned and out-manoeuvred; eventually, straddled by shell bursts, she had to fall back and seek support from our destroyers. As soon as we heard and saw the gunfire through the mist, we cast off our tow lines and increased speed to eight knots. Despite the inevitable circling, this was preferable to remaining still and a 'sitting duck'.

Although considerably outgunned, *Foresight* and *Forrester* immediately went in at high speed to attack the German destroyers. On *Edinburgh* we still had one of our 6-inch turrets operating under manual control. But the ship could not be manoeuvred, and the guns could only be fired as they came to bear as we completed one of our circular gyrations. However, open fire we did and there followed a somewhat wild and intermittent battle as ourselves and the German ships raced in and out of the snow squalls and smoke screens laid by both sides. As we completed another circle, bringing the bows round to face the enemy, the guns in 'B' turret were ready and waiting. Director control was out of action, and the turret was being controlled locally by Lieutenant Howe, standing with his head and shoulders out of the turret hatch. He gave the order to fire, and with an enormous ear-splitting crash the three 6-inch gun muzzles spat out their long tongues of flame and black smoke, and off went three 100-pound high explosive shells towards the leading German destroyer, *Hermann Shoemann*.

The shooting was remarkably accurate, and the salvo fell within yards of the enemy ship. In desperation she tried to turn away towards her own smoke screen, heeling over at an alarming angle. It was a forlorn attempt, and even as her own guns replied, those of our 'B' turret thundered out with another salvo which this time found its mark with a massive explosion which tore the ship apart. With engine rooms destroyed and all control systems out of action, the *Hermann Shoemann* drifted to a stop. This piece of sharp-shooting on the part of Lieutenant Howe altered the outlook completely, and incidentally later earned him the D.S.C.

Meanwhile, *Foresight* and *Forrester* were also steaming rapidly in and out of the snow showers and smoke screens, engaging the enemy ships when they were spotted. Both of our destroyers sustained substantial damage, and the Commanding Officer of *Forrester* was killed in the action. At one point the bridge party on *Forrester* looked on in horror as two torpedo tracks were spotted heading straight for them. The torpedoes passed under them, missing the keel by inches and heading off in the direction of *Edinburgh*, which was slowly completing another circuit and bearing round directly into their course. One of the torpedoes, nearing the end of its run, was slowly splashing along on the surface when it met *Edinburgh* dead centre on the port side. Once again the ship shuddered and lifted in the enormous explosion. We knew it was the final blow, as the hit was immediately opposite where the first torpedo had struck on the starboard side the previous day. The ship was all but cut in two, and we expected her to break into two parts at any moment. However, 'B' turret was still undamaged and was able to continue firing for some time, a number of near misses being recorded. Our damaged destroyers also scored a number of hits on the enemy. Meanwhile, the minesweepers were playing their part in our defence, darting in to attack with guns firing. In the cloud and flame of battle, the enemy supposed they were destroyers arriving to reinforce the British ships; this mistaken supposition restrained them from mounting further attacks. With the *Schoemann* completely disabled and another destroyer badly damaged, the Germans broke off the engagement; after taking survivors off the *Schoemann*, they scuttled her and retired towards Kirkenes in Norway, damaged, dismayed and somewhat disillusioned.

Reports from our damage-control parties confirmed that there was very little holding the ship from breaking in two and going down with heavy loss of life. The Admiral gave the order, 'abandon ship', and at the same time signalled two of the minesweepers, *Harrier* and *Gossamer*, to come alongside to take off the wounded, some passengers who were on passage back to the U.K., and finally the crew.

Harrier and *Gossamer* secured alongside and evacuation of the ship began. It was a difficult process, as the three ships, tied together, rose and fell in the swell. The decks of the minesweepers were 10 or 12 feet below *Edinburgh*'s deck; thus transferring the wounded on stretchers was a nightmare in the freezing Arctic wind and with decks covered with sheets of ice. There was no panic, but there was a sense of urgency since everyone realised that about 700 people had to somehow get on to the two small minesweepers without delay before *Edinburgh* broke up and took her final plunge. There was some trouble getting the evacuees to go below on boarding the minesweepers. Understandable enough; there were U-boats about and if an overcrowded minesweeper were to be torpedoed, everyone wanted to be on deck and not down below.

When the wounded and passengers were all disembarked, it was the crew's turn; every man for himself. I went to the starboard side of the ship, where *Gossamer* was tied alongside, and looked down. I didn't much care for what I was looking at. The two ships were wallowing up and down and backwards and forwards on the swell. One minute they were six feet or more apart and the next bumping together. The minesweeper's deck, some 10 feet below, was completely covered with people staggering about, trying to keep their feet in the swell. There was not an empty space on the deck. Strapped to the side of *Edinburgh* was a large kedge anchor whose shank was about six feet long. I reckoned if I could climb over the side onto this and work my way down the anchor's shank, I would be nearer to the minesweeper's deck. The trouble was, the anchor was completely covered with a layer of ice.

However, I had little option, so over the side I went, embraced the icy shank of the anchor like a long-lost brother, and slid down it until I reached the flukes at the bottom. There I crouched, hanging on grimly, hoping the erratic movement of the ship would not dislodge me from my icy perch and drop me down between the wallowing ships. I soon realised I could not stay in this position for long. I had no gloves and I was literally holding on to bare ice. My hands would soon be frozen and I would no longer be able to hold on. I looked down; someone on the deck below was shouting at me to jump. I tried to gauge the movement so that the ships would be together when I let go …

and jumped. When I reached the deck below it was still crowded with people and as I landed, I flattened about four unfortunates who were in my path. A bit of bruising, but no bones broken. After the colourful language which this episode caused had subsided, someone helped me to my feet and I made my way towards a door leading to the interior of the ship.

Because my action station on *Edinburgh* had been below decks where it was warm, I did not have warm clothing and was clothed only in a shirt, trousers and plimsolls when I left the ship. With the icy blast of the Arctic wind outside, I lost no time getting below when I reached the deck. The small minesweeper was crammed with people, both on deck and down below. Having managed to get inside, out of the freezing wind, I was then able to find a small storage locker, empty except for some cleaning gear, brooms, buckets etc. and squeezed myself into it. There I stayed, afraid to move out for a second in case my place was taken by someone else. I heard someone say, 'What about the gold?' The reply was unprintable. Eventually the commotion of people trying to get off the big ship onto the small one subsided, giving way to the commotion of the minesweeper casting off and trying to get away from *Edinburgh*.

Having disembarked everyone who could be taken off, the two minesweepers, together with *Foresight* and *Forrester*, stood off to watch *Edinburgh* go down. However, contrary to expectations, she did not break up; she just sat there, low in the water, rising and falling in the swell. It was decided to sink her by gunfire. *Harrier* fired about 20 rounds of 4-inch shells. This had little effect except to start a couple of fires. Two patterns of depth charges were then dropped alongside, but this was also unsuccessful. All this noisy activity was not lost on the survivors crowded down below in the two minesweepers; we had not been informed immediately of what was happening, and concluded that another German attack was taking place, and that we would all be drowned like rats in a trap. Calm was restored when we were told that efforts were being made to sink *Edinburgh* by our own forces. Finally, *Foresight* fired her one remaining torpedo, which cut the ship in two in a blinding flash of flame and smoke; and she was gone, taking with her 57 men inside the hull. In all it had taken four torpedoes and a rain of German and British shells to send her to the bottom. The time was 9 a.m. The date was 2nd May 1942. Round about the same time, the *Hermann Schoemann* was settling into her last resting place on the ocean floor with the bodies of those killed on her.

As the morning wore on, the two forces withdrew, the Germans towards Kirkenes in Norway and the British towards Murmansk in Russia, each leaving their dead and carrying the dying and wounded. It had been a furious naval engagement in which there had been neither victor nor vanquished, neither winner nor loser. Both sides had lost a ship, but at least the convoy which we had set out to protect did get through, which gave cause for some satisfaction with the outcome.

Chapter 4

Castaways in Arctic Russia

Early the following morning, the little fleet of destroyers and minesweepers with the Russian tug reached the Kola inlet, where the wounded were disembarked at Murmansk and the remaining survivors at Polyarnoe and Vaenga, two small towns almost opposite one another on the Kola inlet just north of Murmansk.

The minesweepers had to refuel before proceeding up river, and it was nearly 10 o'clock on the evening of 3rd May before they docked alongside the wooden jetty at Polyarnoe. The survivors disembarked and the *Edinburgh* ship's company mustered on the shore for roll call. All we had was what we stood up in. Everything we owned had gone down with the ship. Someone on *Gossamer* had given me a blanket which I wrapped round myself, but it didn't seem to give much heat as I stood trying to get some shelter from the snow showers. The outlook seemed bleak, standing there looking at the snow wastes stretching away to the distant pine forests. We had been fighting the ship for days on end, with little time for food or sleep, and fatigue and the stress of battle were beginning to tell; but at least we were now on 'terra firma' again.

With the stress and strain of battle and the prospect of being blown to kingdom come any minute suddenly removed, a sort of reaction set in, with mixed emotions. I remember wondering why I should be standing there without a scratch after all we had been through, when a lot of our mates were now either lying at the bottom of the ocean, or at best lying dismembered or mutilated and waiting to be patched up in a Russian hospital. It was an odd feeling. A great feeling of relief and thankfulness and indeed disbelief that I was once again standing on dry ground and unscathed, mixed with a deep feeling of unease, weariness and sadness at the loss of both our ship, which had been our home, and so many of our mates. In retrospect, when I heard the armour-plated hatch to the after H.A.T.S. slam shut after the first torpedo struck, I really never expected to see daylight again. After that, I was never again surprised at anything that happened.

It was a slow process, calling the roll and noting the names of the missing, some of them our best friends. When the roll call had been completed, the stentorian voice of the Master-at-Arms rang out, calling the ship's company to attention. In the silence which followed, Captain Faulkner climbed to a little piece of higher ground nearby, where he stood us at ease and addressed us. It was a sad moment. It was not the time for long speeches. He thanked us for the courageous way we had defended the ship and all we had done to try to save it. We were told that this was the last time we would be together as a ship's company. We were to be split into two groups after the injured had been taken to Murmansk. One group was to remain in Polyarnoe and the other one would re-embark on *Gossamer* and go to Vaenga, a few miles further up the river. There was a small British naval base at Polyarnoe which served a small fleet of British submarines stationed there. While the naval base officers would do everything possible to supply our needs, they were entirely in the hands of the Russians, who themselves were living in sub-human conditions. We would have to stay in camps provided by the Russians until such time as we could be transferred in small groups to ships going home. The captain then wished us luck, saluted and walked away.

I was in the group to go to Vaenga, so we re-embarked in *Gossamer*, proceeded up river and disembarked for the last time at Vaenga. We had to march several miles through deep snow to the wooden huts which had been provided for us by the Russians. By the time we got there we were very cold, tired and hungry. The huts were about 150 feet long and 20 feet wide. Each had a platform about 15 feet wide and 2 feet 6 inches high running the length of the hut. A second platform was staged about five feet above the first. These platforms could accommodate quite a number of bodies lying head to head on the bare boards, and this was where we lived for most of our stay in Russia. We were issued with one blanket each. Each hut was warmed by a pipe stove at one end, on top of which was a large cauldron of chlorinated boiling water. This was the only water which was safe to drink.

Jottings of a Young Sailor

After all of our recent exertions, the stress of battle and loss of our ship, an overwhelming weariness took over and we all lay down on the bare boards and fell fast asleep. I don't know how long we slept. It must have been all of 12 hours. I remember awakening and thinking I was in a nightmare until someone spoke to me and asked if I was hungry. I suddenly realised I was ravenous and asked if there was any food to be had. We were told that there was food available at the local communal feeding hall, which was about half a mile away from our hut. With visions of a hot cup of tea and bangers and mash or some such Naval delicacy, we lost no time in getting ourselves up and under way for the feeding hall.

We found it to be a large timber building filled with long timber tables with forms alongside. We were each issued with an enamel bowl and a wooden spoon, and then queued at one end of the hall to be issued with our meal. From the end of the queue it was not possible to see what we were being given to eat, but I did notice that those at the top of the queue, who were taking their filled bowls to the tables to sit down, did not look overjoyed as one might expect after several days without much to eat. When it was my turn to be served I found out why. My proffered bowl had ladled into it a glutinous lump of steaming, ill-smelling, semi-solid grain of some sort. It looked like black barley. After a couple of spoonfuls my hunger left me. I found my reaction to this fare shared by most of my mates, and since there was nothing else on offer, we decided to defer satisfying our hunger until the next meal, in the hope that something more appetising would be available.

However, such hopes were soon dashed when we arrived for the next meal and found we were served with the same dish; except that this time the consistency was that of a watery soup in which, if you were very lucky, you might find a miniscule piece of reindeer meat. The taste was pretty awful, but by this time we were becoming really hungry. I began to realise the meaning of the old saying that 'hunger is a good sauce'. Before long, all of us were eating this 'black barley' at every meal in one form or another, because there was simply nothing else to eat. No meat, no vegetables, no proper bread, no butter, jam, cheese or anything which could be called basic food. Nothing but 'black barley'. At times we were able to obtain a loaf of rye bread, but there was no such luxury as butter, or even margarine or anything else, to put on the bread. It was bitter to taste and impossible to stomach unless toasted. Someone found an old-fashioned coiled-spring electric radiator, and we carefully preserved this and used it only to toast the occasional bread we obtained to make it palatable. The only drink available was boiling water from the steaming cauldrons in the huts or dining hall. Very occasionally, we had the luxury of raisin tea. This was made by putting boiling water on raisins and sultanas (I still don't know where they came from on the Arctic coast of Russia). It was slightly more palatable than ordinary hot chlorinated water. This was our only fare during our three month stay in Russia. We got used to it and survived.

When we left the ship we had brought nothing with us except the clothes we stood in. Since that time I had managed to 'scrounge' a sheepskin jacket to help keep warm and a pair of sea boots to replace my plimsolls, which were fairly useless with feet of snow lying everywhere we went. We had no basic articles like toothbrushes, razors, scissors etc. It was not long before we became quite scruffy, with long hair and beards, and I remember being surprised to find that my beard turned out to be bright ginger!

One of our problems was washing our clothes, because we had nothing to change into. There was a communal wash house with plenty of hot water, baths, wash tubs and soap. It was a large hut with one huge room in which everything took place.

Bathing, washing clothes, drying, ironing, the lot. Since we had nothing to change into, we went into the hut, which was quite warm inside with all the hot water, steam etc., took all our clothes off to wash both the clothes and ourselves, and then had to wait for our clothes to dry before being able to dress ourselves. While waiting, we sometimes amused ourselves by going outside and diving naked into the snowdrift piled up against the steps outside the hut. Very invigorating! This procedure, which was repeated from time to time as occasion demanded, was watched with much amusement by the local populace – both men and women – who also used the same wash house.

The question of how we were going to get back to the U.K. was exercising our minds quite a lot, and all sorts of wild plans were discussed. The trouble was, we were not the only survivors stranded in north Russia. There were literally thousands of Royal Navy and Merchant Navy personnel. It eventually became clear that the only way we could get back was to take passage in a ship. This was not an option any of us were happy about. There were plenty of ships going back to Iceland – both warships and merchant vessels – but the fact of the matter was that most of them never made it but got sunk on the way.

In the meantime, the cruiser H.M.S. *Trinidad*, for whom we had transported the steel plates on our last trip from the U.K., had been patched up well enough to put to sea. She was to return to Iceland with an escort of destroyers, and about a hundred survivors were to take passage in her. Most of the passengers were to be *Edinburgh* survivors, mainly comprising our Royal Marine contingent. I was not included in the draft and could not make up my mind whether to be disappointed or pleased. On the one hand it was an opportunity to get away from this forlorn location and return home, but on the other hand it was an extremely hazardous journey to contemplate. Still, *Trinidad* was a heavily armed ship and should be well able to defend herself if attacked. Since I had missed the draft and could do nothing further about it, I decided to forget the matter.

The 'first aid' repair to *Trinidad* meant she could not exceed 20 knots; but this was considerably better than if she had been escorting an eight-knot convoy. Two of the destroyers escorting *Trinidad* were *Foresight* and *Forrester* – themselves severely damaged in their gallant attempt to protect *Edinburgh* – so it was a case of the crippled helping the crippled. A couple of days into their voyage this small fleet came under withering fire from a combined U-boat and aircraft attack. *Trinidad* was hit by four 500 pound bombs and went down with heavy loss of life. The destroyers managed to escape and later met up with a covering force of British cruisers from Iceland who escorted them safely home.

The loss of so many of our mates with the *Trinidad* did little for our morale. We began to wonder whether we would ever get back to the U.K.

As the weeks went by, we began to get used to our spartan existence, and found that the worst problem of all was boredom. We had nothing to do. There was a large flat area of snow outside the hut we lived in, which was about the size of a couple of football pitches. In order to warm us up and keep fit, P.T. was organised every morning out on this flat area, which soon turned into hard-packed snow. Someone got hold of a ball and football was organised; this was one of our favourite pastimes. Some of us put the time in by walking. We would go for long walks in the snow, mostly through the forest or in the country away from habitation, so that we could keep clear of the many military installations, gun emplacements etc., scattered around the area.

It was only ten or so miles behind the Finnish front, at which heavy fighting was a daily occurrence. Any building of military importance, whether a gun emplacement or a simple farmhouse, usually had an armed guard, normally a somewhat trigger-happy Russian soldier. We found by experience that it was better to keep well away from these individuals, as they were prone to shoot first and ask questions later. On one occasion when out walking, we climbed to the top of a low hill. Below us on the other side of the hill, we saw an airfield with Hurricane fighter planes landing and taking off. This was of interest to us, as some of the merchant ships we had previously escorted to Russia were carrying Hurricane fighters sent up to help the Russian war effort. It was interesting to see them in use. However, while we were sitting in the snow watching the movement of the planes, a Hurricane suddenly flew fairly low over the hill towards where we were sitting. Whether the pilot mistook us for enemy agents or not we will never know, but he circled round, flew straight towards us and opened fire. I remember seeing a dotted line of machine gun bullets in the snow, racing up the hill towards us. I have never seen half a dozen men move so quickly. We made a mad dash for cover amongst the rocks on the hillside. Luckily no one was injured, but we did not linger much longer in the vicinity of the airfield.

Football, baseball and other games became a daily occurrence; until one day when the thaw came we discovered that the flat area we had been using as a playground was in fact a frozen lake. All of a sudden our playground disappeared, and that was the end of football and other such games.

When the thaw came, it came rapidly. The temperature rose slightly above freezing point and stayed there. This caused all the ice and snow to melt and had an extraordinary effect on the landscape. Our playground rapidly turned into a lake; steep snow-covered hills in the village suddenly became rushing torrents of melt water. The trees in the surrounding pine forests suddenly shed their mantle of snow. Previously snow-covered timber walkways connecting one part of the village to another, apparently resting on the surface of the snow, were revealed to be standing two or three feet above the ground. One of these walkways went across a flat area which became a sodden swamp when the snow melted, and we noticed thousands of frogs emerging in the melt water. Presumably they had been hibernating in the snow during the winter. We amused ourselves by catching the frogs, lining them up on the walkway, and racing them along the wooden boards. Some of them were slow starters until prodded in the rear end with a stick!

Nearly every building in the little village of Vaenga was built of timber. Even the civic buildings were made of wood. There was also a very ornate timber-built community centre with quite a large auditorium which doubled as a cinema. I remember going to the cinema one night and being surprised to see an American-produced film called *100 Men and a Girl*. It featured Deanna Durbin as a young vocalist singing with an orchestra of 100 men. The dialogue was in English, with Russian subtitles.

One day we received a piece of good news. The C.W. candidates amongst us were to go before a selection board chaired by our captain, Captain Faulkner. If we passed through this board we would then go before an Admiralty board in the U.K., before proceeding to the officer training school. This was all based on the assumption that we were able to get back to the U.K., which seemed a pretty big assumption at the time. At this point there appeared to be very little prospect of ever getting away from Russia. Even if passage on a returning ship were obtained, it was no guarantee of reaching home, as a high proportion of returning ships were lost before getting as far as Iceland.

Because the Captain and his officers were located in Polyarnoe the selection board we were to attend was to be held there. The half dozen of us involved were told that we would be transferred there more or less permanently. All this brought a welcome change to our somewhat boring daily round. All of a sudden we had something to look forward to. We would have a change of scene. Polyarnoe, although not large, was a Russian submarine base. There were a couple of British submarines based there, and we would have the chance of meeting the crews. All sorts of wild ideas started circulating of maybe getting a passage home in one of the subs. Also, we started thinking about the coming interview at the selection board. Normally these selection boards were very formal affairs and one was expected to be presentably – indeed immaculately – turned out. We were still wearing the same clothes in which we had gone into action. I didn't even have a full uniform. I had a British sailor's tunic, a Russian sailor's cap and a pair of battered sea boots. I hadn't shaved or had my hair cut for six weeks, and looked more like a pirate than a well dressed British seaman. Luckily I was not the only one in this shabby state, and it was with some misgivings that my companions and I arrived in Polyarnoe and presented ourselves at the Captain's selection board, where we were interviewed individually.

The Board consisted of the Captain and his senior officers. My interview went quite well. I was asked numerous questions about the workings of the ship, not only on matters of seamanship, but also about the management of messing and supply, and since I was in fo'c'sle division I was asked to describe in detail the operation of moving the portion of anchor chain from fo'c'sle to quarterdeck during the towing operation after our stern had been blown off. This I had no problem doing, since I had been a member of the party doing the job.

The Captain complimented me on the knowledge I had picked up since joining the ship a relatively short time ago, and said he was recommending me to the Admiralty board in the U.K. There was no indication as to how I was to get there, although he did express the hope that if and when I did, I should look a little more presentable than at present; a sentiment with which I concurred!

Passing through the selection board gave a boost to our flagging morale, as it meant another step completed in our officer training programme. Whilst at sea we had wondered if we would ever see a selection board, because the ship was so busy and never in harbour more than a day or so. The Captain had more pressing matters to contend with than setting up a selection board. Now, if we ever got back to the U.K., we could proceed with the next phase of our training before having to go to sea again.

Polyarnoe, although not very large, was a slightly more civilised place than Vaenga. It was a naval base, had a number of stone buildings and did not look quite as desolate a place as Vaenga. We were housed in a large barrack-like building in rooms which held 10 people in five double bunks. Relative luxury compared with conditions we had recently come from, although the food was no different. The 10 people in our room were in the charge of a Petty Officer who was a born leader and soon had us working as a team; out foraging for food or anything else which might be of benefit to the team. Someone might 'find' an item of clothing, someone else a tin of beans. We were always on the lookout for food, and at one stage discovered the food store which supplied the few British naval ships which visited the port. It was not long before 'visitations' to this store were organised and various odd items of dry stores – such as a tin of beans or canned fruit or a jar of jam – were purloined for the common good. Eventually, nearly every day someone in our room would come back with some item of swag. It became a sort of competition amongst us as to who could do best at this 'game'. Everything brought back was carefully rationed and divided out between us, and I remember a jar of jam being shared out each evening, one small spoonful each per day until it was finished. Same thing happened with a tin of peaches, two slices each per day. These little luxuries reminded us of how well off we had been before landing in Russia and heightened our desire to get away from the place.

We were always on the lookout for food or some way of obtaining it. One day a new possibility presented itself. A British minesweeper came alongside in the port to replenish supplies, and some of us were detailed to a working party to help load some of the supplies onboard. Much to our delight, we discovered that some of the supplies consisted of crates of butter and (of all things) casks of rum. Very rapidly, devious plots and schemes were worked out to enable a little of this precious cargo to be suitably 'misplaced'.

The butter was an easy matter. This was contained in wooden boxes which held maybe a stone of butter in one pound blocks wrapped in grease proof paper. Picture a line of half a dozen men walking down the quayside from the food store to the ship, each carrying a wooden box on his shoulder. While passing an old crane on the quayside, one of the men trips on a piece of chain on the ground and drops his box, which splits open and spills its contents on the quay. The man hastily gathers up the spilt contents and tries to replace them in the broken box, helped by some of his mates who gather round to assist. In the confusion some of the blocks of butter get 'misplaced' under an old piece of canvas covering the back of the crane. The damaged box is eventually carried on board with apologies for its state and the fact that a few blocks may have got lost in the 'accident'. The 'lost' blocks are retrieved and taken to our room in the barracks later in the evening, after all activity on the quay has ceased and the coast is clear.

The rum seemed a much more difficult and risky matter. We knew an armed guard would be on the quay to discourage and ward off any attempt to interfere with the rum supply. The rum was contained in stone bottles, each of which was enclosed up to the neck in a wicker basket with a woven cane handle on each side. I suppose each bottle would hold about one gallon. The cork in the mouth of each bottle was sealed with red sealing wax impressed with the Admiralty seal. The bottles contained full strength, undiluted Jamaica rum. To obtain one of these bottles would indeed be a real coup for our scavenging team!

The plan was surprisingly simple, if it would work. Since each bottle was quite heavy and there were plenty of hands, the bottles were walked along the quay from store to ship by two men, one on each handle of the bottle. We noticed that whereas a close eye was kept on the full bottles, easily distinguishable by the large red seal on the top, the empty bottles (with no seal or cork) being returned from the ship to the store in similar fashion were not so closely watched. We also noticed that although there was a guard on the door of the spirit store on the ship, watching the full bottles going in and the empty ones coming out, there was no one actually inside the store. How easy it was for the pair detailed to do the job, having entered the ship's store with the full bottle, to quickly remove the seal and cork and walk out again with the same bottle as if it were an empty one and walk back down the quay past the guards to the quay store. Before reaching the store, the bottle was 'parked' amongst a pile of old oil drums near the store, to be collected later. This coup was celebrated in our room in the barracks for many weeks to come by the issue of a small tot of rum to all hands in the room each evening.

There were two British submarines based at Polyarno; H.M.S. *Trident* and H.M.S. *Seawolf.* A friend and myself visited these subs when they were in port after a patrol, and became very friendly with some of the crew. Hearing about our privations ashore, the crew took pity on us and occasionally invited us to a meal on board. This was extremely generous of them considering that they were very short of basic foods themselves. There is not much room on a submarine to store food, or anything else for that matter. Needless to say, these very occasional meals on board were highlights of our stay in Russia. What luxury to enjoy a piece of white bread and a cup of tea! Both things we had not seen for weeks. As time went on, we even began to hope we might get a passage home on one of the subs, being about the safest means of transport at the time from Russia to Iceland. Unfortunately there was no sign of their tour of duty in Russia coming to an end. Although they went on patrol around North Cape, they always returned to Polyarnoe and not Iceland.

Chapter 5

Homeward Bound

At last my turn has come. H.M.S. *Volunteer* has docked at Polyarnoe. She is one of the old 'V' and 'W' class destroyers built at the end of World War One, and I have been included in a batch of a dozen survivors drafted to take passage in her back to Iceland. Very mixed feelings. It is now July. Midsummer. It is daylight 24 hours a day in these latitudes.

Jottings of a Young Sailor

Also the weather is usually calm and clear. Ideal for U-boats and aircraft, but not so good if you are trying to dodge them. We try to calculate our chances of making it back to Iceland and don't much care for the answers we are getting. On the plus side there is the fact that we are going independently and won't be held back by escorting a slow-moving convoy, so we can make good speed; maybe 20 knots or more. On the other hand, being independent means no help around if anything goes wrong. We are on our own. Also, the Germans know every time a ship leaves Russia and are out there waiting for us.

Still, the die is cast. We are going, so stop worrying about the risks. A certain amount of fatalism takes over and we go on board and settle in to our new surroundings. Not as spacious as on *Edinburgh*; the ship is less than 30 feet wide, but not as cramped as a submarine. The crew are very helpful and have some sympathy with our predicament. We are glad to learn that we will be given normal seagoing duties to perform, mostly lookout duties. You can never have too many lookouts on duty, especially in these waters. This will give something for our bodies and minds to work on; a welcome change from our erstwhile boring occupation of doing nothing most of the time.

We are on our way. It's great to be at sea again. It's even greater to be back on a British ship and eating food which, if not of gourmet standards, is immeasurably better than we have had for months on end. How one appreciates such simple things as a potato, an apple, a dish of rice pudding or even a cup of tea. The weather is beautiful. The sun is shining. The sea is calm and the temperature is above freezing point. We have left Murmansk behind and are thrashing along on a flat calm sea, zigzagging at 20 knots plus. This could be a pleasure cruise! Or could it? The only reason we are thrashing along zigzagging at 20 knots plus is to make it a bit more difficult for the U-boats, which we know are there, to have a shot at us. A torpedo amidships on

Edinburgh did a lot of damage. A torpedo amidships on this ship would blow it and everyone on it out of the water.

I am on lookout duty in the crow's nest and rather enjoying the novelty of being on a small warship. The *Edinburgh* seems huge in retrospect, and the movement is entirely different here. When the ship rolls on the ocean swell, I look over the rim of the crow's nest and see below me not a ship but the sea.

It is exhilarating travelling at this speed after having been used to the speed of the slowest ship in a convoy. If we continue like this we will be in Iceland in a few days rather than the few weeks it usually takes. Still, Iceland is fifteen hundred or so miles away and a lot of ground (or water) has to be covered before we reach there.

On leaving the Kola inlet we steamed due north as far up as the edge of the ice shelf, which had retreated further north in the summer months. We were able to pass to the north of Bear Island to keep as much distance as possible between us and the Norwegian coast.

We were now steaming west through the ice floes on the edge of the ice shelf somewhere near Spitzbergen. Action stations sounded off. Apparently U-boats were attacking a convoy far to the south of us. We continued on our way at speed. My action station was in the shell room serving one of the 4-inch guns. It was in the bottom of the ship. It was extraordinary how sound carried through the water for long distances. Down in the shell room we could quite distinctly hear the sound of exploding depth charges miles away, as the convoy escort attacked the marauding U-boats. The sounds of battle gradually faded as we drew away, and we were stood down from action stations. No one complained.

We were making good headway towards Jan Mayen Island, which was about 400 miles off the coast of Greenland. Weather was beautiful. Calm and sunny. We were a little nervous about

Jottings of a Young Sailor

U-boats, but at the speed we were travelling they would have a job catching us. The Captain decided to take advantage of the good weather – and the fact that he had a number of spare hands in the form of passengers – to paint ship. I and one of my mates were assigned to paint the forward funnel.

We collected our gear from the paint store. Overalls, paint and brushes, and a stage and lines for lowering ourselves from the top to the bottom of the funnel. I had often worked with a stage when painting ship on *Edinburgh*. A simple but effective piece of equipment; it consisted of a wooden plank about six feet long, with cross pieces about two foot six secured across each end in such a fashion that the ends of the plank stuck out each end beyond the crosspieces. A rope was tied securely on each protruding end of the plank, passed up to the top of the part of the ship being painted (in this case the funnel), through a block (or pulley) and back down again to be secured to the plank end again. Having rigged the stage I sat on one end of the plank (inside the 'fall') and my mate on the other, each equipped with a brush and full can of paint hanging on a hook underneath the plank. We hauled on the fall (the rope going up through the pulley) and pulled the stage to the top of the funnel. We started on the starboard side, the idea being to paint a broad strip down the funnel then move the stage round a bit and paint another broad strip. In this way we worked our way round and down until the whole funnel was covered.

All went well for a while, and we were getting used to the action, which became more tricky as we moved down the funnel. The trouble was that as the ship rolled in the swell, the stage swung out from the funnel. This was no problem at the top, but as we worked our way down, the length of the fall increased and so did the distance the stage swung out when the ship rolled. We found we could still manage by painting furiously while the ship rolled us against the funnel; when we rolled out and the funnel went out of reach, we used this time to replenish the paint on our brushes. As we progressed down the funnel the movement became somewhat alarming, because the lower we moved the longer the fall became and the further we swung out when the ship rolled, and we reached the point where we were well out over the sea beyond the ship's side on every roll. Bearing in mind that a warship at sea in wartime never stops if someone is unfortunate enough to fall overboard, we were not overjoyed with the position we were getting into.

We had progressed well with our funnel painting – having reached about half way down – when disaster struck. A sudden end to our painting occurred when the fall at the opposite end to my own parted. This had a catastrophic effect. My mate at the other end of the plank suddenly found himself in mid air and plummeting down towards the deck. He landed with a sickening thump, having had his fall broken on the way by a deck locker and a coil of hawser wire, which did little to soften his landing. Nevertheless, in a way he was fortunate that the ship happened to be rolling in the direction that deposited him on the deck. If the roll had been in the other direction he would have landed in the sea. A softer landing perhaps, but he would have been lost. As it was, although somewhat bruised and shaken, he had no bones broken and soon recovered. The commotion of his landing from aloft soon produced a crowd of matelots from nowhere, who concentrated on ensuring he had no broken bones and helping him to the mess deck where he could recover.

Meanwhile, when the plank suddenly upended, I had made a wild grab for the fall at my own end and held on for dear life! The result of the other fall giving way was, apart from depositing my companion on the deck, that my own fall, with the plank and myself suspended on the end of it, started gyrating around the funnel like a ribbon round a maypole, keeping time nicely with the roll of the ship. I remember thinking at the time, 'This is real

Jottings of a Young Sailor

Laurel and Hardy stuff!' My roars and shouts for assistance had the effect of transferring the attention of the people below from my mate on the deck to myself gyrating round the funnel. A Petty Officer appeared on the scene and enquired in rather flowery naval language why I was 'playing silly buggers swinging round the funnel'. I replied that I would be only too happy to tell him if he would only get me down before I was catapulted over the side of the ship! Someone eventually rigged an improvised ladder up the funnel, came up and grabbed one of my legs as I swung past on one of my wild gyrations. It was with some relief that I was then able to let go the rope I had been clinging to and climb down to the safety of the deck. That ended our painting activities for the day.

Next day I found myself on lookout duty on the Bofors gun platform. Still brilliant weather, bright sun and blue sea, although a wind had arrived and there were white caps on the waves. We were still speeding along at 20-plus knots, which gave one a great sense of security. I didn't know whether it was misplaced or not. At least we felt that if there was a U-boat commander looking at us through his periscope, our speed would make it a bit more difficult for him to hit us. I suddenly noticed that the sea had changed colour. The deep blue of the Arctic Ocean had gone a sort of pale blue colour; nearly green. I was discussing what the cause of this might be with another lookout on the gun platform when there was a cry of 'land ahead!' from the masthead lookout in the crow's nest. We all looked forward and saw that we were charging headlong towards a coastline three or four miles away which stretched as far as one could see in both directions. At the speed we were going, it wouldn't take long before we were running ashore!

Luckily the Officer of the watch on the bridge became aware of the position and ordered a 90-degree turn to port, which at 20 plus knots meant our heel to starboard during the turn was such I thought we were going to capsize. We eased a little further from the coast into deeper water and realised that the land along which we were travelling was the northeast coast of Iceland. It was not long before we arrived at Seydesfjord. We steamed slowly up the narrow fjord and anchored at the head, close to the little town, at a spot where we had often anchored in *Edinburgh*. We noticed that there were some other Naval vessels in the anchorage, including one of the latest 'M' class destroyers, H.M.S. *Martin*. This ship had only recently been commissioned and created much interest amongst the crew of the much older *Volunteer* on which I was travelling.

It was only an hour or two after arriving at Seydesfjord that we learned that the *Martin* was leaving the next day for the U.K., and was going to take some passengers. Imagine our delight when we later learned that all of the passengers on *Volunteer* were to be transferred to *Martin*. At long last there was some prospect of returning home. It was too good to be true after our fast but rather perilous passage from Murmansk. England was still a thousand miles away down the North Atlantic, and a lot could happen in those waters but we felt we would be relatively safe in one of the Navy's newest and fastest destroyers. We could hardly have picked a better ship if we had had the choice. With a top speed of 35 knots, she could cover the distance home in a couple of days if travelling unaccompanied. We were not told whether we would be going alone, but it was unlikely to be otherwise unless we had to escort something like a submarine or cruiser.

Next morning, amid great excitement and anticipation, we took our leave of the *Volunteer* and transferred to *Martin*. After the endless waiting in north Russia, things now seemed to be happening very rapidly. We had no sooner boarded our new home and settled in than the familiar sounds of preparations for putting to sea started, and we were under way back along the fjord towards the coast. The passengers on this trip were not allocated any shipboard duties as had been the case on *Volunteer*, where we had become temporary members of the ship's company. We were solely passengers and not required to do anything except keep out of everyone's way.

A very fast and uneventful passage took us to our first sighting of land, which was the island of Rockall, far out in the Atlantic off the west coast of Scotland. It was a brilliant sunny day and as we passed within about half a mile of the island, the gunners on the Pom-Pom deck let off a few practice rounds. This caused the island's population of thousands of sea birds to rise in a squawking mass, swirling around us in noisy protest at our intrusion into their domain.

Less than 24 hours later we were steaming up the Mersey to Liverpool; the whole trip from Iceland having taken about two days. This was a very fast time. Even in *Edinburgh* it used to take us two days at least to get to Iceland from Scapa Flow, which is a lot further north than Liverpool.

As soon as we docked in Liverpool the passengers were disembarked and taken to a survivors' reception centre, where at last we were given all the care and attention we needed. Firstly a medical examination, then to a clothing store where we were kitted out with everything from the skin out. It was like having a shopping spree without having to pay for anything. Having been washed, clothed and fed in short order, we were then put on a train to our home base, Devonport.

Devonport barracks, or H.M.S. *Drake* as it was called, had not changed. Only we had changed since we left the place about nine months ago. Having survived the sinking of our ship and three months stranded on the north coast of Russia with little or no food, we no longer felt like raw recruits and were not treated as such. In many ways, Devonport barracks was like a huge manpower warehouse, but it had a certain efficiency about it, dealing with the daily comings and goings of hundreds of personnel of different categories and ranks. As survivors we were rushed through the system. Firstly a medical examination, followed immediately by a fortnight's survivor's leave. This was not recorded in one's pay-book, which meant it was not counted against you when qualifying for your next leave.

A couple of days after arriving in barracks I was on my way again, this time on a train to Heysham to catch the ferry to Belfast and home. My parents were on the quay in Belfast when the ferry arrived and there was a joyful reunion, following which we drove to Bangor in County Down, where my home was at that time.

Needless to say, the fortnight's leave was a happy time. In retrospect the thing most remembered is the immense feeling of relief at the sudden removal of the threat of sudden annihilation which was present at sea. In wartime a ship is in the front line the moment it leaves the safety of harbour.

It was a joy to have the simple things of life again. Sleeping between clean sheets, enjoying the simplest of foods like bread and butter, jam, fruit, sugar etc. It is only when one has done without such things that their benefit is really appreciated.

The fortnight's leave passed all too quickly and I found myself once again entering the gates of H.M.S. *Drake*. Since first entering that establishment I had learned a lot about the ways of the Navy, and now did not feel as much like 'an innocent abroad' as I had then.

In the Navy in wartime, leave was something you got only when circumstances permitted – which wasn't very often if you were at sea. Most naval ships, with the notable exception of capital ships like battleships, were almost constantly at sea, with very little time in harbour. Hence one only got leave if one's ship was in dock for refit or if one was changing ship and passing through barracks. I well remember on shore leave at Scapa Flow the animosity – and sometimes drunken fights – which arose between crews from cruisers and destroyers (who would, if lucky, have a couple of days in port) and crews from battleships like H.M.S. *George V* which seldom went to sea.

When returning to barracks, having been at sea for at least three months, one was always entitled to 'back from sea' leave (usually a fortnight) before going back to sea. When I returned to H.M.S. *Drake* after my survivor's leave I immediately applied for back from sea leave. I was granted a further fortnight. My parents were therefore a little surprised to see me back on their doorstep again a few days after I had left! In the Navy you learn to take what you can get when you can get it, so I had another two weeks' sojourn in luxury at home.

On returning to *Drake* after my second leave, I learned that I was shortly to go to H.M.S. *King Alfred* in Hove. This was the officer training school on the south coast of England. Since the powers that be did not know when I was to go, and didn't know what to do with me at *Drake*, I was sent off on indefinite leave! This not only surprised my parents when I arrived home yet again, but surprised me a little too. Still, who was I to object to another unexpected spell of home leave?

It was now early October 1942. I was three weeks into my indefinite leave when I received orders to report to H.M.S. *King Alfred*, a shore establishment at Hove, outside Brighton in the south of England. It was used by the Navy at the time as an officer training school. I arrived on 3rd October 1942 and spent the remainder of the month there, completing the officer training course before passing out with the exalted rank of Sub Lieutenant R.N.V.R.! Having passed out and been commissioned, I was interviewed by the Training Commander at *King Alfred* and asked which branch of the service I would wish to be posted to. I replied that I had only one wish and that was to go back to sea. Here the old bogey of my defective eyesight again raised its head. I wore glasses. The Navy does not like sailors who wear glasses. Because of this I was precluded from any job which involved watch-keeping at sea. Other seagoing jobs were few and far between. The Training Commander thought I could probably get to sea by being posted as an officer in charge of the armaments on a large merchant ship, so I agreed to this.

My future having been thus settled I was again sent off on indefinite leave to await a posting. After about three weeks I was called back to a further Officer Training Course at the Royal Naval College at Greenwich. At the time this establishment was run as a Naval university and it was considered quite an honour to be sent there. Why I was included in the chosen few from the hundred or so who had just passed out from *King Alfred*, I never knew. However, my stay there, which lasted about a month or so, was one of the most enjoyable times of my Naval service.

In the reign of King William III of England, Greenwich College, one of London's famous buildings and a Baroque masterpiece, was designed by Sir Christopher Wren, the architect of St Paul's Cathedral. The foundation stone was laid in 1696 and the building took 50 years to complete. It was originally built as a Naval hospital but from 1873 was used as Naval College, continuing in that role until 1998.

It was now late 1942. In England, food was rationed and some everyday items like butter, tea, sugar etc. were extremely scarce. Luxury items like cooked ham, turkey and tomatoes were practically unobtainable. Yet here we were, living like kings in this palace. Dining each evening in the magnificent Painted Hall, sitting at the long oak tables with silver candlesticks and cutlery, eating venison, goose, roast lamb or beef every night while the Royal Marine band played softly in the minstrels' gallery. I couldn't help but think how my fortunes had changed from what seemed like a short time ago when I was scrounging around for a piece of bread to eat outside Murmansk in north Russia.

It was during my time at Greenwich that I had the unforgettable experience of being caught out in a real 'pea soup' London fog. At this time such things as air pollution and global warming had not yet come into vogue. In certain atmospheric conditions the pollution from numerous chimney emissions was trapped in the air over the city and formed a dense, impenetrable fog. It could be so dense that one literally could not see the ground one was walking on.

I remember leaving the college one afternoon to go up to London to visit Madame Tussaud's wax museum. I had heard about this museum but never seen it. Having spent two hours or so inside, I came out to be met at the entrance by a 'pea souper' of a fog. It was strangely quiet for London, as all traffic had stopped. No cars, buses or trams. The only thing still operating was the underground. With some difficulty I made my way to the nearest underground station and boarded a train to New Cross Gate on the Old Kent Road, which was the nearest station to Greenwich College at the time. When I left the train and climbed up the steps to the Old Kent Road, I again could not see the ground and wondered how I was going to reach the college, which was one or two miles down the road. It was a peculiar sensation. Buildings, lamp posts and any form of landmark were all invisible. It was like being completely blind. Then I had a flash of inspiration. I knew trams normally ran down past the college. If I could get out to the middle of the road I could follow the tram lines down the road with my feet. No fear of being knocked down as the fog was far too dense for the movement of any traffic.

The problem was to get to the middle of the road. With some difficulty I managed to negotiate the few yards' width of the footpath and reached the kerb. In the eerie silence I took off at right angles from the kerb, walking slowly in what I thought was a straight line towards the centre of the road. Having left the kerb, which was my only point of reference, I soon lost all sense of direction. I knew if I walked straight I would eventually reach the tram lines, so I proceeded slowly, carefully putting one foot a short distance in front of the other. After a while I thought it was time I should have reached the tram lines. A moment of panic! Had I gone round in a circle and missed them? Should I alter course and go a bit further to the left or right? No, keep going straight. I plodded on, thinking that if I went straight, the worse that could happen would be I would reach the other side of the road. But if I crossed the road I must meet the tramlines because I knew they were there.

After what seemed an age, wonder of all wonders, I felt my foot touch the tramline. I brought the other foot up so that both feet were in the rail. What a sense of relief and security. At last I knew where I was – at least relative to the road. But I still had to walk about a mile down the road to reach the college. I started walking along the rail, which I found quite easy to feel with my feet, so that I could keep up quite a brisk pace, knowing that I was going in the right direction. I was congratulating myself that this was all too easy when I was brought down to earth with a jolt by my feet suddenly coming to a set of points! One rail went straight on and another went off to the left. Which rail to take? I had not been up and down this road often enough to recall where there was a branch to the left which the trams took. I realised I was lost. I stood there at the points in the middle of the road for some time, wondering whether to turn left or go on. I did not have a clue which way to go, and I think it was some kind of instinct that made me opt for going on straight. Having made the decision, I took off again at a brisk pace along the rail, hoping I did not come upon any more points.

The next problem was deciding how far to go before leaving the tram tracks and taking off to find the footpath at the side of the road. I could only guess when it was time to do this by considering the time I had been walking and the speed I had been going. I reckoned I had been walking for half an hour and that it was therefore time I found the footpath. I did not want to go past the college. It was now pitch dark, with no street lamps in the wartime blackout, and I could still not see the ground. I turned left and stepped out at right angles to the rail, slowly putting one foot in front of the other in as straight a line as I could manage. After what seemed like another age of wondering whether I was going straight or not, my foot eventually struck the kerb and I knew I had arrived at the footpath.

Which way to turn? I crossed the footpath, feeling with my hands for a wall or something solid. I came to some railings in front of what, in the gloom, looked like private houses. While I was deciding whether to go left or right, I heard footsteps. Someone approached from my left holding a torch which was pointed towards the ground, showing a faint glimmer of light in the fog. They passed by to my right and I decided to follow the faint light, thinking that whoever it was they had a better chance of finding their way than I had with no light. I followed the light for a few hundred yards, crossing several side roads in the process, all the while feeling with my hands along the walls and railings at the side of the footpath. I suddenly found myself going along a stone wall about five feet high with high railings on top, and recognised it with relief as the railing around Greenwich College.

I had arrived at last. All I had to do now was follow the wall until I came to the entrance. But my troubles were not over. Inside the entrance I had to cover about two hundred yards of open ground to reach the nearest block of buildings. It was as black as pitch, no lights, and the fog was so thick I still could not see the ground. I had a fair idea of the direction of the nearest building, so set off, walking as straight as I could, on the assumption that if I kept going long enough I must come to some building. As an experiment I tried closing my eyes. As I thought,

Norman Sparksman

I could see just as much with my eyes closed as with them open, which was absolutely nothing. I think I now know something of what it must be like to be completely blind. Eventually I came upon one of the main blocks and found the door by groping my way around the wall. I was much relieved to get inside, but astounded to find that the fog had penetrated inside the building and even with all the interior lights on, I could barely see across the room.

The next day the fog had gone, but I shall not forget my one and only experience of a London 'pea souper'. What impressed me most was the silence. The usual roar of traffic, patter of feet and general noise of numerous people moving about was absent. No traffic could move and the only people about were the few like myself trying to find their way home.

Chapter 6
D.E.M.S.

After my few weeks living in style at Greenwich College, I was sent home again on indefinite leave to await posting. After fourteen days on leave I received orders to proceed to H.M.S. *President III* at Cardiff for a D.E.M.S. Gunnery Officer's course at the gunnery training school there. D.E.M.S. was a division of the Navy which dealt with the arming and supply of defensive equipment on merchant ships. (D.E.M.S. stands for Defensively Equipped Merchant Ships.) During the war all merchant ships carried guns and defensive equipment, the amount on each ship depending mainly on its size.

Ships over 5,000 tons would normally have at least a 4-inch gun mounted aft, with several smaller guns, say 20mm Oerlikons, in other positions. A complement of naval personnel was supplied to man these guns. On very large ships like passenger liners and troop carriers, the amount of armament and naval crew aboard warranted the carrying of a fully qualified Naval Gunnery Officer and it was to train as such that I was sent to Cardiff.

The course, which was very intensive, lasted about six weeks. There were about a dozen other junior officers like myself on the course and we learned the intricacies of naval guns and gunnery. There were lots of practical tests during the course and a comprehensive written examination at the end. I found the course interesting and enjoyable and felt that I had acquitted myself well in the final examination. I was therefore surprised and considerably disappointed to be told, when the results were published, that I, with one other officer, had failed. That the other officer had failed was no surprise to any of us, as all the way through the course it was obvious that he was not going to make the grade. My fellow students were as mystified as myself as to why I had failed, and no reason was given. It would be two years before I discovered the reason.

Feeling somewhat disillusioned and disgruntled, I went home on leave again to await posting, but knew that this was the end of my attempt to return to sea.

After being on leave for six weeks, in February 1943 I was surprised to receive a posting to H.M.S. *President III*, Belfast. (*President III* was the name given to all D.E.M.S bases all over the world.) Although I would not be going to sea as a gunnery officer, use was being made of my gunnery training by posting me as a D.E.M.S. Gunnery Inspection Officer. My disappointment at not getting back to sea was to some little extent tempered by the fact that I had been posted to Belfast, which was only half an hour's train journey from Bangor, where I lived at the time.

When I received my letter of appointment to *President III* Belfast, I noticed that the date of appointment was about ten days prior to my receipt of the letter. This resulted in my having a somewhat frosty reception when I reported for duty in Belfast the day after I received the letter. When I stated that I had only just received the appointment letter, I knew by the reaction that I was not believed. It was not until I was able to produce the Admiralty envelope in which the letter had been posted and which bore the clearly marked date of posting that I was able to convince them that I was telling the truth. Thus my tour of duty in Belfast did not have a very propitious start.

During the war, Belfast was an important Naval base. Besides the construction and repair of Naval ships in the Belfast shipyards, the port itself was in constant use by shipping carrying war supplies from America to Britain. Belfast Lough was a major convoy assembly anchorage for ships of incoming and outgoing convoys to and from America, the Mediterranean and North Russia.

The D.E.M.S. base where I was stationed was housed in a large school. It had been commandeered by the Navy and was used as a barracks to house the naval ratings who manned the guns on the merchant ships which visited Northern Ireland. It also housed the staff of Inspection Officers who serviced the ships visiting the port. There were about a dozen of us, headed by an R.N.R. Commander. The barracks and the inspection staff were under the overall command of an R.N. Captain. Most of the time I was in Belfast I was responsible, along with another officer, for covering the ships which were at anchor in Belfast Lough. The two of us each operated a commandeered Scottish fishing drifter from the docks in Belfast to visit the hundreds of ships anchored in Belfast Lough. Each day I would travel by train up to the D.E.M.S. base in Belfast, then go down to the docks, board my drifter and steam back down the Lough to visit the ships anchored off Bangor. It was not long before it dawned on me that this routine was a waste of time in the extreme, as I spent far too much time travelling to where I was working. I suggested to Captain D.E.M.S., who was the commanding officer of the D.E.M.S. base in Northern Ireland, that it would be more efficient if we were to open a D.E.M.S. office in Bangor, so that I could operate my drifter from there and thus be that much closer to the ships I had to visit in the Lough. Much to my surprise he said, 'Yes, good idea, go ahead and open an office in Bangor.'

At the time Bangor itself was quite an important Naval base, serving the needs of the hundreds of ships constantly assembling in Belfast Lough for convoys. The Admiralty had taken over the Royal Hotel in Bangor, and this was the headquarters of the S.N.C.O. (Senior Naval Control Officer). As the base grew, the hotel was not large enough to house all of the Naval staff required, and additional premises were acquired on Queens Parade on the sea front; it was here that I was able to persuade the S.N.C.O. to give me a couple of rooms to set up a D.E.M.S. office.

I staffed the office with a Chief Petty Officer and another naval rating, and moved my drifter from Belfast to Bangor harbour. This arrangement worked very well. I was now able to cycle from my home in Bangor to my office and be at sea off Bangor in a matter of ten minutes. A great saving of time over the previous routine.

I remained in this post for two years, during which time I became intimately involved in the work of servicing the hundreds of Allied ships which visited Belfast Lough. At times there would be as many as 400 ships anchored in the lough at one time. Each one of these ships had to be visited, and since they seldom stayed for more than a few days while their convoy assembled, we had a busy time getting round them all before they departed. I operated from Bangor and covered the ships at the seaward end of the anchorage, while my colleague, another D.E.M.S. officer, operated from Belfast with his drifter, covering the ships anchored further up the lough at the Belfast end.

It was interesting work, although the hours were long. All ships had to be visited and we sometimes had to work half way through the night to get round them all before a convoy left. It was energetic too. The only way aboard the ships was up a 50- or 60-foot rope ladder on the ship's side. In bad weather with a strong wind blowing it was something of a struggle while carrying a briefcase.

Ships visiting the anchorage were of all Allied nations, so we met people of all nationalities. Since we were helping them by supplying the needs of their defensive equipment, we were usually welcomed aboard but we soon became used to differing attitudes towards us and never quite knew what reception to expect. Some elderly Captains looked upon a very young Naval Sub Lieutenant as something of an upstart and treated me as such; whereas others took a much more fatherly attitude.

British Naval crews manned the armaments on most Allied ships – except American vessels, which were manned by their own Naval crews. The average merchant ship might carry a Naval crew of six gunners in the charge of a Leading Seaman or Petty Officer. They would be responsible for maintenance of the defensive equipment – normally consisting of a 4-inch anti-submarine gun and a number of smaller anti-aircraft guns. It was my job to inspect this equipment to ensure that it was properly maintained in a state of readiness for action, and that the gun crews were properly trained and exercised ready for action. On most ships the Second Officer assumed overall responsibility for the defensive equipment, and it was this officer I usually visited when calling on ships, having first called briefly on the Captain as a matter of courtesy.

Sometimes my reception was a little more hearty than was good for the work to be done. Some of the captains seemed pleased to have someone from ashore to talk to, and I sometimes had difficulty escaping from their hospitality to get on with the job. Most of them were all too liberal with the spirit bottle and at times it was not easy to avoid becoming a little inebriated before leaving the ship, especially when half the time one was not aware of what one was drinking.

On one occasion, when visiting a Greek ship, the Captain, who did not speak English, welcomed me cordially with his Chief Officer, who did speak English. I was bidden to sit down in his cabin. A steward was summoned, was given a brief order in Greek, and soon returned with a silver tray on which stood six glasses filled to the brim with colourless liquid. Three of the glasses were half pint tumblers and the other three were a smaller size. I was not even asked whether I wanted a drink, but being the guest was offered the tray first. I was a little puzzled as to what to do but after a little quick thinking surmised that I was supposed to take a large glass and a small one. I was somewhat relieved to find the Captain and his First Officer did the same. So far so good, but what to do with the two full glasses. I reasoned I should wait for the Captain to make the first move, which he did. Lifting the smaller glass up, he said something in Greek which I took to be 'good health' or something similar, swallowed all of its contents and then swallowed half the contents of the larger glass. Not knowing what I was in for, I dutifully followed suit with the First Officer. I immediately discovered that the small glass contained neat gin and the large one nothing worse than cold water! Could have been a lot worse, I thought.

The officers on many of the ships visited were so pleased with the service we were providing that they plied us with gifts on our leaving their ships. These gifts were usually bottles of wine, cigarettes or tinned food of some kind, which was scarce ashore due to wartime rationing. The cigarettes were invariably American and consisted of a carton of 200 (10 packets of 20). I received so many cigarettes that I had sufficient for not only my own use but also to supply my drifter crew and half the officers in my section of the Naval base. One of the officers I kept in cigarettes was the local senior customs officer, who happened to be a personal friend of mine! A smart move, that. I always had one or two thousand cigarettes in my D.E.M.S. store on my drifter. The customs officer always gave me warning before he made his periodic raid on all of the Naval drifters in Bangor harbour so that I could move my cigarette stock temporarily to my office while the raid was on!

One day, while steaming down Belfast Lough, I was sitting in the wheelhouse alongside the skipper when we spotted something floating in the water in our path. On slowing down to investigate we found a batch of cigarette cartons. American cigarettes were packed in cartons of 200, the cartons themselves being enclosed in waxed paper to keep them watertight. We stopped the drifter, and the crew, armed with shovels and boathooks, fished more than two dozen undamaged cartons aboard – 5,000 cigarettes; not a bad haul for just a few minutes fishing! We could only conclude that someone on one of the many ships at anchor had dumped the cigarettes out of a porthole window on the approach of a customs officer. My customs officer friend was very amused at this story when I told him a couple of days later. Customs were not unduly worried about me taking cigarettes off ships and giving them to my crew and friends. What they did object to strongly – and did everything to stop – was people getting cigarettes from ships and selling them on the black market.

Working on the ships in the anchorage was very interesting, and because many of the ships we serviced returned again and again after their various voyages, we got to know the officers and crews quite well. The Naval Officer on one American ship which called at Belfast Lough regularly was the film actor Douglas Fairbanks Jnr, whom I came to know very well. Because of rationing ashore, food was very scarce and I was frequently invited to stay on board for a meal if I happened to be there at mealtime. This happened on ships of all nationalities, but it was particularly welcome on the American ships because they never had the shortages of food experienced by their European allies. I was invariably wined and dined when Douglas Fairbanks' ship arrived. Another ship which was a regular visitor was a Spanish vessel. Although Spain was not at war, Spanish ships sought the protection of British convoys. We always welcomed the sight of this particular ship, as we knew we could obtain a couple of bottles of port, sherry and Spanish wine.

One of the services I provided for the convoys was to organise a practice shoot for the ships' gunners when the convoy left Belfast Lough. I had a target made which consisted of a wooden raft with a flagpole on it, which I towed a couple of hundred yards behind my drifter. The convoy ships fired their 4-inch guns at it in turn as they left the anchorage entrance. With perhaps as many as twenty or more ships in a convoy, the operation had to be carefully planned and the ships' captains briefed on the procedure to be followed. I would carry out this briefing at the convoy conference which preceded the sailing of all convoys. One of the main safety regulations governing all practice shoots was that no gun must fire unless the black flag was flying on the control boat, which was my drifter. In practice, no matter how careful the planning and the briefing, something usually went wrong.

Normally practice ammunition would be used for these shoots. Practice shells were the same size as live shells but instead of being filled with high explosive they were filled with salt, so that when they landed they did not explode. One problem was that American ships did not have practice ammunition. At first we would not allow them to take part in the shoot, but later relented under pressure and agreed to their participation. We lengthened the target towline a bit to get the towing drifter further away from the target. Some of the shooting was erratic, to say the least, and some of the high explosive shells were exploding uncomfortably near the drifter at times. On one occasion there was consternation in the convoy when the first ship to open fire, which was an American, scored a direct hit on the target with his first shot. Since he was using live ammunition, the shell exploded and blew the target to smithereens. None of the remaining ships had an opportunity to fire as there was no longer any target. After that incident we always carried a spare target but never again had need for one.

On another occasion at a practice shoot, an American ship started shooting at my towing drifter instead of the target. Luckily he was firing with a 20mm Oerlikon gun and not a 4-inch gun. Nevertheless, the 20mm shells were high explosive and could be very lethal. The cook on our drifter was a rather simple-minded man, and I found him gleefully counting the 20mm tracer shells passing over the galley roof of the drifter. I dashed out of the wheelhouse and told him to get below, and at the same time signalled the firing ship to cease firing – which he did with some reluctance.

The crew on the drifter were of course experienced Scottish fishermen and had a trawl which they had rigged up for fishing in their spare time when I was not using the craft for Naval purposes. Sometimes after a practice shoot we would find ourselves half way across the Irish sea by the time 20 or more ships had had a few shots at our target on the way out. On finishing the shoot and drawing the target up close behind the drifter, we would drop the trawl and do a bit of fishing on the way home. This resulted in my having an ample supply of fresh fish to distribute amongst my colleagues in the Naval base at Bangor and also to my mother and her friends at home.

Practice shoots had to be very carefully organised to ensure safety. With perhaps 20 ships firing off at a target over a period of an hour or two it was essential to ensure that the range behind the target was always clear of either passing ships or land. Practice shells hitting the water at a low angle could ricochet for miles before coming to rest and sinking. Failure to observe this rule could have dire results, as a colleague of mine in the Naval base in Belfast found out to his cost. This officer was in charge of a party of ratings on a practice shoot taking place on a Naval auxiliary ship off Bangor one day. They were about five miles offshore at the mouth of Belfast Lough, firing at a towed target with practice shells fired from a 4-inch gun. The relative positions of the firing ship and the target changed, so that the coastline at Bangor came into line behind the target. When this happened the Shoot officer should have stopped the firing immediately, but failed to do so. The result was that a practice shell, missing the target, carried on ricocheting across the water all the way to Bangor, crossed the seafront road, bored its way through the front wall of a seafront house, carried on through the front room of the house past a man sitting reading a newspaper, bored its way through the back wall of the house and eventually came to rest in the back garden! Needless to say, this episode made headline news in the local newspapers with such headlines as 'Bangor bombarded by Naval gunnery training ship'! The officer concerned, who was known amongst his trainees as something of a martinet, never lived the event down and was the butt of many jokes for years afterwards.

During the time I was stationed in Belfast Lough I was doing a lot of sailing in my spare time at Ballyholme Yacht Club. We raced every Tuesday evening and Saturday afternoon, and I crewed in one of the Ballyholme Bay Class boats whenever

H.M.S. *Edinburgh*

Captain Faulkner (left) & Admiral Bonham-Carter

Foc'sle Ice, H.M.S. *Edinburgh*

Hermann Shoemann on fire and sinking

Jottings of a Young Sailor

H.M.S. *Harrier* taking *Edinburgh* survivors

Greenwich College

Norman Sparksman

Painted Hall, Greenwich College

Jottings of a Young Sailor

I was able to be off duty at race times. I eventually bought my own boat, one of the 'Bay' class, and named her *Gossamer* after the minesweeper which had rescued me from the *Edinburgh* at the time of her sinking.

One of my friends in Bangor, George Crowe, had joined the Fleet Air Arm; after his training as a pilot he was stationed at Sydenham airfield in Belfast at the same time as I was stationed in Bangor. He was flying Fairey Swordfish torpedo-carrying planes, and was often spotted flying around Belfast Lough when on duty at Sydenham. He too was a keen yachtsman and sailed in the same class of yachts as myself. Like me he always raced if off duty but sometimes, when on duty on a race night, he would fly down from Belfast to watch the racing from the air. The Swordfish were slow, rather cumbersome biplanes, and he would zoom around us at about fifty feet, giving us a wave as he flew past. In calm conditions, when there was little wind for sailing, he would sometimes fly up and down close behind a yacht of his choice to create an artificial wind and so give that yacht an advantage over its competitors, much to the chagrin of the latter.

After the war George married a girl who lived next door to my home and set up home himself in Bangor, appropriately enough calling his house 'The Rookery'.

All the convoy activity entering and leaving Belfast Lough on a daily basis was not lost on the Germans, who were constantly looking for ways to stop or hinder it.

U-boats had difficulty getting into the Irish Sea, owing to British naval patrolling of the northern and southern entrances. Because of British air supremacy they likewise could not mount air attacks during daytime. They did however manage to sneak in night-time mine laying aircraft on a couple of occasions. Magnetic mines were laid in the anchorage and main channel to Belfast.

Norman Sparksman

On a sunny Sunday afternoon in midsummer I was off duty and walking along the seafront at Bangor, watching a merchant ship entering Belfast Lough. It was a ship called S.S. *Troutpool*. As she steamed past Bangor towards the anchorage further up the lough, I saw an enormous explosion and a cascade of water spouting up around the ship. She had passed over a magnetic mine which blew the bottom out of the ship. As I watched, the ship just settled and went straight down until she was sitting on the bottom of the lough with her masts and superstructure still above water. (During the two years or more I spent at Belfast this was the only ship lost to enemy action.)

The *Troutpool* went down in the middle of the channel to Belfast port and constituted a major navigational hazard, so immediate steps were taken to move the wreck. Using flotation gear she was lifted and moved at high water to Ballyholme beach at Bangor, where she was broken up for scrap. After this incident, Belfast Lough was swept continuously for magnetic mines which might be laid at night by aircraft, and a boom was placed across the entrance to prevent submarines from entering under cover of darkness.

Merchant ships crossing the Irish sea frequently flew barrage balloons from their mastheads. Originally, large kites were used, but these gave way to balloons, which were more stable. This was a defence against dive-bombing aircraft, a very effective and accurate form of bombing employed by Germany at the time in all theatres of war.

There was stationed at Bangor a Naval officer whose title was 'Kite and Balloon Officer, Belfast Lough'. His duties were to supply and fit balloons to ships requiring them and to take balloons off ships no longer requiring them. During my time at Belfast, 'My Lords of the Admiralty' in their wisdom decided to remove this officer from Belfast and send him somewhere else, despite the fact that he had plenty of work to do, with

Jottings of a Young Sailor

ships flying balloons coming and going regularly. Not only was the officer removed but he was not replaced and no one (who mattered) was told about it. The first I learned about it was when my phone rang at two o'clock one morning, when I was in bed. It was the Senior Naval Control Officer in Bangor, who informed me that a ship flying a balloon had just entered Belfast Lough and was leaving the next day for America, and needed the balloon removed. 'But I'm not the Kite and Balloon Officer, sir,' I protested. 'We haven't got one, and you're the next best thing, get out there and get the b—y thing off,' he replied. In true Naval fashion I was thus pitch forked into the role of Kite and Balloon Officer, Belfast Lough, despite the fact that I did not know one end of a balloon from the other.

The K and B officer was never replaced during the remainder of my time at Belfast, and because my prompt removal of that balloon in the middle of the night apparently satisfied the powers that be that I was capable of doing the job, it was dumped in my lap. In retrospect, the additional duties were not very onerous and did not unduly interfere with my other D.E.M.S. duties. The only problem was that I had no trained staff, and had to do everything connected with balloons myself – including going up to the mastheads of ships, sometimes in the middle of the night, to remove balloons.

Whilst at sea a ship would fly its balloon from the masthead, on the end of a 500-foot steel wire. On entering harbour the wire, which passed to the deck through a pulley block on the masthead, would be wound in until the balloon was 100 feet above the mast. At lower heights than this the balloon became unmanageable, especially if there was any wind blowing (which was most of the time). To remove the balloon from the ship, someone had to climb to the top of the mast, undo the shackle securing the last 100 feet of wire, tie on a lanyard carried up from and secured to the deck, and bring down to the deck the end of the unshackled steel wire. Because I had no one to do this operation for me I had to do it myself. After having done it a few times, I became quite adept at going up masts in all sorts of conditions. However, on a cold wet winter's night with a gale blowing, it was not one of my favourite pastimes! When the end of the flying-off wire was secured on deck, the balloon, now with a lanyard tied to the end of the last 100 feet of wire, would be manhandled over the side of the ship to my drifter, which was tied alongside. It took three men to hold the balloon down and walk it to the ship's side. One man alone would be lifted off his feet, so we always made sure three people were holding on to the lanyard until it was safely secured to the drifter.

Sometimes a convoy of a dozen or more ships carrying balloons would cross the Irish sea and arrive in Belfast Lough together, and I would have more balloons than I could cope with. When this happened I called for assistance from my colleague operating the other drifter from Belfast. This resulted in two drifters festooned with three or four balloons each, making repeated trips in to the central pier in Bangor; much to the interest of the local population. We had to deflate the balloons on the pier. I then stowed them on my drifter until a slack day, when I would take them up to Belfast to a balloon store in the docks there.

Belfast Lough was not a good anchorage when the wind was in a northerly quarter. A gale inevitably resulted in some of the ships in the anchorage dragging their anchors; if uncontrolled this could have dire consequences as the anchorage was crowded most of the time.

On one particular occasion, a Danish motor ship, the M.V. *Oregon 1* came into the lough with engine trouble. She anchored far up the lough with the intention of proceeding to Belfast the next day for repairs. That night the wind increased to gale force from the northwest and her anchor started dragging. Her engines could not be started and by morning she had dragged across the anchorage to Bangor, and was only a few yards off the rocks at Wilson's Point. As the gale continued, those of us ashore could only look on helplessly as the ship eventually struck the reef and broke her back. The local coastguard rescue team managed to get the ship's crew safely ashore, and the ship was left to her fate. Knowing that the ship had a 4-inch gun and other defensive equipment on board, I used the day of enforced inactivity to organise a working party in readiness to board the ship as soon as the weather moderated.

The wind did not ease until the following day, and even then there was still a heavy swell breaking over the stricken ship, which made getting alongside and boarding a dangerous operation. However, the ship had broken her back and I knew that if we did not salvage what we could without delay, we would soon lose the chance of getting anything off. With my working party aboard my drifter, we managed, with some difficulty, to manoeuvre alongside the after portion of the ship as it heaved up and down on the swell. I scrambled aboard with my party of sailors and promptly started dismantling the guns and equipment and assembling everything we could on deck for transfer to the drifter, which for the time being was told to stand off into deeper water and await instructions.

Later, another party from the armament store in Belfast arrived and between us we managed to get the large 4-inch gun removed from its mounting and transferred, with most of the smaller items, into the waiting drifters. The only item we could not remove was the gun mounting which, weighing several tons, was too dangerous to move without heavy equipment which we did not have available. All the while these frantic efforts were proceeding, the unmistakable sounds of a ship dying were in our ears. The grinding and tearing of metal, the bumping of the ship's bottom on the rocks below, and the cracks like pistol shots as steel girders and plates snapped below under the strain. Eventually we had everything off that we could get off and I made a final tour of inspection. As I was about to leave the ship for the last time, I noticed a small cannon on a wooden carriage mounted on the roof of the ship's bridge. I climbed up to take a look, scraped off a little of the thick layer of grey paint with my penknife and found that the barrel was brass and the carriage made of oak. This was not a working gun but more of an ornament. It seemed a pity to leave it to be lost with the ship, so I took it home as a souvenir. When cleaned up it turned out to be an old eighteenth century gun which had probably passed down a line of ships with the same name. It reposed for some years outside the front door of my parents' house in Bangor until it was presented to Bangor Borough Council in 1962, for a local museum which the Town Clerk was establishing at that time.

On the evening of the following day, I walked round the shore to where the shipwreck had taken place. The sea was calm. A light breeze rippled the water and the sun setting over the Antrim hills on the other side of Belfast Lough cast a sort of golden hue over the scene. The *Oregon 1* lay there, in two pieces about fifty yards apart. Once a proud ship, now just two pieces of useless rusting scrap. Having been shipwrecked myself, I could not help thinking of the Danish crew who had a couple of nights ago so desperately scrambled ashore, leaving all their belongings behind, who were now stranded in a foreign land, their only possessions the clothes they stood in.

Having been in Belfast Lough for more than two years, during which time I seemed to be continually taking on more and more additional jobs, my responsibilities had increased considerably over those I had when I first arrived. Also it was now nearly three years since I had received my last promotion to the rank of Sub Lieutenant. I considered the work I was doing and my three years' seniority warranted promotion to the rank of Lieutenant, so I broached the matter with my Commanding Officer in Belfast. I was pleasantly surprised to find he was quite prepared to plead my case with the powers that be. However, I was told that the regulations required five years' seniority for an officer under 30 years of age, and since I was 24 at the time I did not have a hope. Such are the ways of the Navy. My C.O. in his recommendation pointed out that all of the other officers at Belfast who were doing similar duties to myself held the rank of lieutenant, but it was of no avail. I had to soldier on, albeit somewhat disgruntled.

Chapter 7

Abroad Again

Whether my agitation for promotion had anything to do with it or not I don't know, but not long afterwards I had a phone call one morning from my C.O. in Belfast. He was a man of few words, and without preamble of any kind said, 'Sparksman, you're going to India.' At this stage I had been in the Navy long enough not to be surprised at anything that happened, so I merely replied, 'Oh yes, sir, when?' Not immediately, I was told. I had to go and do a course first. This did not surprise me either, as in the Navy one always had to 'do a course' before changing jobs. It appeared that I was to be trained as a Gunnery Instruction Officer, because there was a shortage of such officers in India. Once I got over the shock of suddenly realising that the work I had been doing for the last couple of years was going to end, I became quite enthusiastic about the prospect of travelling to India and getting some knowledge of what was then a far-off land. The proposition was all the more attractive because my long-awaited promotion had arrived. I would be promoted to Lieutenant on being posted.

In due course my posting came through and I went off to Cardiff in South Wales, to the same gunnery school I had trained at before I went to Belfast. This time I was to be trained as an instructor. I already had the gunnery knowledge but now had to learn how to teach others.

On arrival at Cardiff I found nine other officers had arrived to take the same course as myself, all bound for India. We were all a little surprised. Ten gunnery instructors for India. What on earth were they going to do with us all out there? Still, who were we to question the decisions of 'My Lords of the Admiralty'?

A couple of days after arrival, when we had settled in, we were all interviewed individually by the Training Commander in charge of the school. It was the same officer who had been there the last time I was there. He remembered me from the previous course and greeted me affably enough but what he then told me incensed me so much, I could have cheerfully throttled him on the spot. Recalling my last course at the school he said, 'Yes, you were on the course training as a seagoing D.E.M.S. officer. We could not possibly let an officer wearing glasses go to sea.' I felt like asking why he had not told me that two years ago, instead of merely telling me I had failed the course! Or for that matter why I was not told before I started the course. What was the point of the course if I was failed before starting? Such are the ways of the Navy.

The instructors' course lasted a number of weeks, after which we were all sent home on indefinite leave to await posting. In due course my posting arrived; to H.M.S. *President III*, India. Report to Dock Number 10, Liverpool.

In 1945, almost all travel was by sea or rail; hardly anyone went by air. On entering the dock shed at Liverpool I found it full of Service personnel of all kinds. Hundreds of people, milling around and queuing up at various desks. Eventually I found a desk with a queue of Naval people and on closer approach came across the other nine officers who had been on the course with me in Cardiff. There were very few Naval people, only about 20 altogether, so that we were 'processed' fairly quickly and were then ready to embark. Most of the passengers were army people, but there was a large contingent of about 200 W.A.A.F. (Women's Auxiliary Air Force), some 50 of whom were officers. The fact that we were to have some female company on the passage made the anticipation all the more.

When we passed out of the shed onto the quayside I looked up and saw something which looked like a steel skyscraper with portholes. I had never seen such a huge ship. During the war, the names of ships and their destinations were kept very strictly secret, so that we had no idea what ship we were to travel on. It turned out to be the new *Mauretania* which, at the time, was the largest ship afloat next to the *Queen Mary*. She had been converted to a troopship.

We filed on board and were allocated cabins. The cabins had been refitted with six two-tier bunks in each, with a bathroom adjoining. I was in an outside cabin, so that there were two portholes which gave us daylight and a view of sorts. The ten of us who had been on the course in Cardiff were in the same cabin. After settling in we went for a walk around. The ship seemed enormous, with so many decks and corridors it was easy to get lost. The public rooms were still very luxurious. The main dining room was huge, spanning the full width of the ship, beautifully furnished with both large and small tables. The Naval officers were allocated two adjoining tables, seating 10 each. This was 1945 and we had been through six years of wartime austerity. We could not help thinking that if the food on board matched the surroundings we were in for a pleasant surprise. Was this going to be a pleasure cruise?

Our first meal in the dining room was an eye-opener. It was like a first class hotel. We were handed a menu containing all sorts of foods we had not seen for years and regarded as luxuries. Cooked ham, bacon and eggs, coffee, cream, tropical fruits, etc. etc. We learned that the ship, which crossed the Atlantic regularly, provisioned in America where all types of food were abundant. I had not seen such a plentiful supply of good food since my brief stay at Greenwich Naval College. Understandably, the dining room was filled to capacity at every meal – at least it was before we put to sea.

It took most of the first day to check everyone on board, but at last the job was completed, the shed cleared and all the gangways except one removed. We were ready to sail. But sail we did not; not today, not the next day or the day after. There was a gale blowing outside and the ship could not get out of the dock into the river. The gale continued for a week while we wined and dined in the lap of luxury and enjoyed ourselves with the various on-board activities. We were not in the least worried about the delayed departure. It was like a pleasure cruise and there were few, if any, complaints.

At last the wind decreased sufficiently to allow us to move. From the boat deck we watched with interest the tricky manoeuvring with the aid of tugs to get this huge ship out of the dock with very little room to spare. Out in the river the wind was still quite fresh and cold, so we went below to the warmth of the interior.

The *Mauretania* did not sail in convoy, but relied on her speed to avoid U-boats. On leaving Liverpool we turned northwards in the Irish sea and proceeded round the north coast of Ireland into the Atlantic, then due west for about 500 miles before turning south for Gibraltar. As a westerly gale had been blowing for a week, there was quite a rough sea running in the Irish Sea when we got outside. The ship started rolling and there were noticeably fewer people in the dining room for dinner that night.

By the time we got up next morning we had rounded the north coast of Ireland and met the full force of the Atlantic swell, which had built up during the week's storm. When a gale has been blowing for a week in the Atlantic, a long deep swell develops, with the waves reaching 50 to 60 feet. There is a lot of movement even on large ships, and the *Mauretania* was no exception. For a few days, as we made our way down the Atlantic towards Gibraltar, conditions were uncomfortable to say the least. It was not long before the only tables in the dining room occupied at mealtimes were the Naval ones. However, such conditions have an advantage, and that is that it makes the U-boats' job of aiming torpedoes more difficult. Knowing this, and also knowing that this part of the Atlantic was infested with U-boats, the Naval types on board were not sorry to see the rough seas, and were able to give some consolation to the landlubbers who were suffering somewhat because of the weather conditions.

After a couple of days in the rough Atlantic, we turned eastwards and entered the Mediterranean. There was still quite a swell but not so pronounced as in the Atlantic. Also it was now much warmer and we were soon able to change into tropical gear. The dining room became more populated again at meal times. Life on board became much more pleasant as the sea calmed and blue skies appeared. Sunbathing and deck games became the order of the day as we proceeded at full speed down the Mediterranean Sea towards the Suez Canal.

A few more days found us anchored off Port Said, waiting to disembark some of our passengers and for passage through the canal. When we went on deck and looked over the side, we found the ship surrounded by a fleet of 'bumboats' plying their wares. These were the local traders, selling everything from all sorts of exotic fruits and flowers to locally made trinkets of ivory, wood or basket. These bumboats swarmed around every ship that arrived like wasps round a jam pot. Since most of us were in transit and did not know where we would end up, and had a limited amount of baggage, we had little incentive to purchase souvenirs at this stage. Had we been on the way home it might have been different. As it was, the traders eventually got the message that there was not a lot of business to be had at the *Mauretania*, and most of them left, apart from a few hopefuls who hung on until we weighed anchor to proceed through the canal.

At that time the *Mauretania* was the largest ship ever to go through the Suez Canal, and we had to wait until all other shipping had been cleared before we could enter. For most of us on board, our arrival at Port Said was our first view of the East. The Royal Air Force personnel all disembarked at Port Said and we said our goodbyes to the W.A.A.F. officers, whom we had come to know fairly well during the passage. The outer decks of the ship were crowded with passengers, all eager to get a view as we proceeded through the port to enter the canal.

Passage through the canal on this huge ship was an unforgettable experience. As the canal passes through the desert, it is an extraordinary sensation, travelling through endless expanses of sand dunes on an ocean-going ship, with nothing but sand as far as the eye can see in all directions. The canal was so narrow that the ship was literally pushing the water in front of it as it went along. A wall of water could be seen being pushed up out of the canal and flowing over the sand alongside, then cascading down into the canal again behind us as we went along. At one point I was somewhat startled by the sight of an ocean-going ship two or three miles away, apparently sitting in the sand in the middle of the desert. As we rounded a bend in the canal we came upon the ship lying alongside a wharf. At intervals along the canal are passing places where the canal has been widened and a wharf built so that a ship can tie alongside to allow another ship going in the opposite direction to pass.

After passing through the town of Ishmailia, about half way through the canal, we proceeded via the Bitter Lakes, which form a large part of the southern end of the canal, to the port of Suez at the southern end, about one hundred miles south of Port Said. During the passage through the canal the heat seemed oppressive after the cool breezes of the Mediterranean, and this heat was to stay with us for the remainder of our passage to India. We were beginning to get a taste of what it is like living in the tropics.

Another 200 miles brought us out of the Gulf of Suez into the Red Sea, which is more than a thousand miles long, then across the 2,000 miles of the Arabian Sea to Bombay (Mumbai) on the west coast of India. It had taken a total of 11 days since leaving Liverpool, at that time a record-breaking passage.

The ship arrived at Bombay in the middle of the night and anchored a couple of miles offshore. The first we knew of our arrival was when we awoke one morning to a most peculiar and unpleasant smell. Someone who had been in India before informed us that it was 'the mystic smell of the East'! I remember going on deck and looking across the mile or so of sea towards the shore. All manner of craft were scattered across the calm water; other ships lying at anchor, smaller craft ferrying back and forth from ship to shore, and numerous small boats and sampans. On looking over the ship's side there was the inevitable swarm of bumboats trying, without much success, to sell their fruit and trinkets.

It was calm, not a ripple on the water. The sun bore down from a cloudless sky and the heat seemed like a weight on one's shoulders, and this odd smell permeated everything. It was like a mixture of perfumed flowers, spices, sweaty humanity and animal dung. As we stood on deck wondering what was before us when we went ashore, the klaxon horns blared and an announcement informed us that we should proceed to our cabins and await instructions for disembarkation. This surprised us a little, since we were still anchored some way offshore and were expecting to dock somewhere to disembark. However, we learned that there was no dock large enough for the *Mauretania* so disembarkation would be by tender, ferrying us ashore.

The remainder of the day was taken up by the tedious process of disembarkation. Endless queuing and waiting for our turn to board the tenders which came alongside both port and starboard. I suppose each tender carried about 200 passengers. Eventually our turn came and we walked out through the side of the ship onto the stairway down to the small tender below. It was with some reluctance that we left the ship, as we had enjoyed the voyage, which had been something of a pleasure cruise for us, with food the likes of which we had not seen for years.

It took about half an hour to reach the shore, and it seemed that the nearer we got, the more intense became the heat and the smell. The heat was so overpowering that every breath seemed to burn the lungs. I remember wondering how on earth I was going to survive such a climate. Little did I know that in a couple of years' time I would be standing on the same shore, thinking what a beautiful climate with its gentle fresh breeze blowing in from the sea. Everything is relative.

Norman Sparksman

When we reached shore, the group of Naval officers I was with was conveyed in army station wagons to a transit camp in the hills, some miles inland from Bombay. Driving through and out of the city gave us our first impressions of India and the 'East'.

My first impression was the teeming hordes of people. The only time I had seen anything like so many people at one time was outside a football stadium after the match had finished and all the spectators were streaming out of the grounds into the streets outside. In Bombay it was like that not just in one street but in all the streets. It was interesting just to watch the crowd go by. All sorts. Rich, poor, old, young; and all colours too. I had imagined Indian people to be black and maybe Negroid in appearance, and was surprised to find them very fine-featured, mainly of light build and varying in colour from almost black to almost white, with many shades between. It is a land of contrasts. The grinding poverty of the bare-footed beggars dressed in rags, walking the same street alongside the opulent wealth of the rich trader's wife clothed in a bejewelled sari. The impressive stature of the Sikh men walking past the poor snake charmer at the edge of the footpath with his basket of snakes and pipe wailing. The traffic was chaotic. Cars, buses, bicycles, rickshaws and pedestrians all competing for a space in the overcrowded thoroughfares.

The ten of us who had been on the Gunnery Officer Instructors' course were anxious to find out where in India we were going to be posted as Instructors. We were told that all would be revealed when we arrived at the transit camp, where we were to stay for some days until onward transport to our final destinations was arranged.

The transit camp we found to be a collection of mud huts thatched with palm fronds. The walls were all whitewashed inside and out, and the buildings were arranged in the manner of a military camp, with parade ground and flagpole in the centre. We were allocated a cabin each, which was adequately furnished with a bed, wardrobe , chair and table. Meals were served in a larger hut which served as a dining room. The officers' mess was a large hut complete with bar, lounge-chairs and tables etc. We were pleasantly surprised at the relative comfort of the accommodation, which was something better than we had been expecting.

I remember walking into the mess on the first evening and the first thing that caught my attention was the unusual decoration on the whitewashed interior walls. A sort of stippling effect. I had not been in the mess long before I discovered how this effect was produced. It was hot, very hot. There was no glass in the windows, only shutters which were wide open to let in what little movement of air there was outside. Numerous mosquitoes and other insects were buzzing around inside, attracted by the electric lights. When a mosquito landed on the wall the drill was to swat it with a newspaper or something similar. This squashed the blood-filled insect in a little splash of blood on the whitewash. You then took a biro, drew a little circle round the body and added your initials in the circle. There were hundreds of these little circles all over the walls of the mess. This was how the unusual wall decoration was formed.

The morning after our arrival we were at last informed of our ultimate destinations. It appeared that the powers that be were somewhat surprised at the arrival in India of ten new naval gunnery instructors, and did not quite know what to do with us. The upshot was that of the ten officers who had received this special training, one received a posting as a gunnery instructor and the remainder of us were posted to various ports in India as D.E.M.S. Inspection Officers, exactly the same job we had been doing in the U.K. Such are the ways of the Navy.

I was posted to D.E.M.S. Calcutta, given a rail warrant and told to report to the D.E.M.S. Staff Officer Calcutta. It was now

April 1945. No such thing as air travel (at least not for me). The only way to get from Bombay to Calcutta, a thousand miles as the crow flies, was either by boat or train. By sea, the journey took about a week or more, depending on the ports of call on the way. By train the journey took two and a half days. Thus I elected to go by train. The train journey was an education in itself. I was one of only a handful of Europeans on the train. Most of the passengers were Indian army personnel. I was certainly the only British Naval officer and felt something like 'a fish out of water' travelling across the middle of India on a train. The train was the Bombay-Calcutta mail express. It left Bombay, climbed up over the hills and made its way across the middle of India to the busy town of Nagpur, stopping at various smaller towns on the way.

We slept on the train but I was surprised to find that we left it for our meals. At every mealtime – breakfast, dinner and tea – the train stopped and everyone disembarked, went into the station dining room and had the appropriate meal. The organisation was remarkably good. It was really all part of the railway company's operation. The train was a regular one, usually running on time. They knew when it was coming and how many people to cater for and what meal was required. The food was excellent. It was indeed surprising for me in the middle of this very foreign eastern country, with completely different customs and traditions, to be able to enter a dining room and sit down to a typically English breakfast of fruit juice, cereal and fried ham and eggs.

As the train rattled along through the Indian countryside, the journey itself was very interesting and something of a travelogue. We went through mountains, across plains, through cultivated areas, areas of scrubby bush and stretches of dense jungle. All the way there was a sense of an overcrowded and overpopulated country. Even in the remotest areas one could usually spot someone working in a field, cultivating with a rudimentary plough drawn by oxen or water buffalo or gathering fruit from a patch of pineapples. The overcrowding was more pronounced as we passed through villages and towns. Anywhere the train stopped it was besieged by hordes of beggars looking for 'baksheesh' or vendors selling trinkets. It was interesting watching the world go by at these stations.

Apart from the beggars and trinket sellers, the platform would become crowded with passengers getting on or off the train with their baggage. What never ceased to surprise me was the enormous amount of baggage the porters on these stations carried. Most people who travelled around India, myself included, used a tin trunk for their baggage. They were relatively lightweight for their size, and bug-proof, which was an asset in a country where insects were even more numerous than people. The porters, who wore a small round pad on their heads, would stand bolt upright while two of his mates loaded a full tin trunk and several suitcases onto his head. Off he would walk with this enormous load on his head, without the slightest trouble. He was not alone. The station was full of porters carrying similar loads, followed by the loads' owners, who were careful not to let the load disappear out of their sight otherwise they might never again see either their porter or their baggage. Carrying everything on their heads was the custom, not only for porters but also everyone else. The women would carry, on their heads, everything from a small handbag to a large heavy urn of water.

On that train journey two sights are forever etched in my memory. At one busy station, while waiting for the train to restart its journey, I was watching the world go by outside my window and spotted what must have been a butcher's boy. He was hurrying along the platform with a huge basket of meat on his head. In the basket were what appeared to be half a side of beef, several legs of lamb and miscellaneous other large pieces. I remember thinking it did not appear very hygienic in the dusty heat of an Indian afternoon. A feature of most of the country stations along the line was that the platforms had hip roofs over them to provide some shade from the scorching sun. Along the ridge of these roofs was always perched a row of large vultures, carefully eyeing everything going on below in case some tempting morsel of food appeared. As the butcher's boy walked along the platform I watched one of the resident vultures take off and swoop in a long glide down towards him. Gliding across the basket of meat, the bird lifted off a leg of lamb in its talons so delicately that the man did not know it had happened and continued on his way, quite unaware he had lost part of his load. The other unforgettable sight was that of a begging woman walking along outside the train with a not so large basket on her head in which was sitting a small legless child.

Eventually the train came into the more heavily forested and wet country of the Ganges delta, with its numerous rivers, ponds and dense forest. We finally rumbled into Howrah station in Calcutta on the river Hoogly, after our thousand mile journey from Bombay.

After my arrival in Calcutta, a number of things happened in such rapid succession that in retrospect I wonder how I kept up with them at the time. I was met at the station by an officer from the D.E.M.S. base at which I would be stationed, and taken with my baggage to the office, where I was told that my first priority was to find somewhere to live. I was soon to find that this seemingly easy task was something of a problem. During the war, when large numbers of troops were always moving around the world, most cities and large towns had an Officers' Club where one could stay temporarily if in transit or otherwise needing temporary accommodation. I happened to arrive in Calcutta in the middle of a cholera epidemic, and the Officers' Club was full up because the main hotel, the Palm Court, and all other hotels in the city, had been put 'out of bounds' for all service personnel.

The remainder of that day was without doubt the most unpleasant time I spent in India. I was tired after a two-and-a-half-day train journey. I had just arrived in a strange, far eastern country, with an entirely different unfamiliar culture and customs; I didn't know the language, and I had nowhere to sleep that night. I went to what I thought was a residential district of the city and started knocking on doors, looking for a bed for the night.

In 1945 the war was in its advanced stages. The tide had turned in favour of the Allies in Europe and the war there was nearing its conclusion. There had also been significant advances in the Pacific war, where considerable progress had been made in driving the Japanese forces back towards their homeland. At the time I arrived in Calcutta, the Allied advance down the Arakan coast of southeast Asia towards Rangoon was taking place. Calcutta was an important strategic base, through which most of the supplies of war materials and troops passed on their way to this front.

Because of the large numbers of service personnel passing through Calcutta, accommodation was scarce, and the situation was aggravated by the not infrequent cholera epidemics which took place at the time. Many of the residents, English, Indian and Anglo-Indian, opened their homes and took Navy, Army and Air Force officers in as paying guests as a contribution towards the war effort.

When I started knocking on doors looking for somewhere to stay, my reception was varied. In some cases, where the occupants did not speak English, I had a communication problem and had to pass on. Admittedly, these were in the minority. Quite a few would not, for a variety of reasons, entertain the idea of putting me up, even for one night. Then there were those who were not averse to taking me in but had no spare rooms or what spare space they had was already taken. Having spent the whole of the evening searching without result, it came to 11 o'clock and

I was becoming desperate, with nowhere to stay for the night. I remember knocking on one door and explaining my plight to an Indian lady. She was very sympathetic, but informed me that she had only one spare room and that was already taken by someone who was at present away, but would be returning in the morning. Like a drowning man I clutched at this straw and, with considerable difficulty, persuaded the lady to let me sleep the night in the empty bed on condition, I assured her, that I left immediately after breakfast in the morning and paid for laundry of the bed sheets! What a relief! A bed for the night. Tomorrow's another day. Being somewhat tired after the day's exertions, I lost no time getting into the bed. My troubles were over at least for the moment.

The following morning I reported back to the D.E.M.S. office in the docks with all my baggage, hoping that someone on the staff there would be able to help me with my accommodation problem. Indeed there was someone who helped me, but not in the way I expected. It was the D.E.M.S. Staff Officer (my boss). He informed me that I was to proceed to the docks and there board a passenger ship bound for a place called Chauk Pyu on Ramree Island, off the coast of Burma. The officer whom I had been intended to replace in Calcutta had been posted to Chauk Pyu as D.E.M.S. Staff Officer, with orders to establish a D.E.M.S. base there. The officer concerned had taken ill and could not go, so I was posted in his place. At the time, Ramree Island was a beach-head on the coast which Allied forces had recently taken during the advance to Rangoon; it was thus behind the Japanese lines. I was dispatched with a Petty Officer and a party of seamen and told to report to the Senior Naval Officer in charge at Chauk Pyu. From him I would obtain living quarters and the accommodation required to set up a D.E.M.S. office, which would service the ships calling there on their way southward to Rangoon.

Thus my immediate accommodation problem was solved, but I could not help wondering what awaited me and the party for whom I was responsible when we reached Burma.

Off I went again with my baggage, and boarded the ship bound for Ramree Island. I had no sooner gone on board than another problem presented itself. I had now been in India for a week or so, and whether it was the change of climate or (more likely) the change of food, I was suddenly struck by a dose of dysentery. It was a most unpleasant and debilitating complaint which made me feel quite ill. I had sufficient worries already without having to worry if I was going to be physically able to carry out the job I had been sent to do. Luckily the trip to Ramree took two or three days, so I was able to rest in my bunk for most of the way. However, I was still suffering the complaint when we arrived at our destination but by that time had learnt how to cope better with it.

The ship was staying at Ramree Island for a couple of days before continuing southwards on its voyage; so I left my party on board while I went ashore to see what the situation was regarding accommodation. Proceeding towards shore in the ship's boat, all I could see at first was a jungle-covered shoreline. On closer approach a small jetty appeared, but there was little sign of houses or other habitation, and my heart sank. The boat pulled alongside the jetty and I climbed out, giving instructions for the coxswain to call back for me in an hour's time.

Walking up the small jetty I could see no signs of habitation until I went into the trees, where I came upon a somewhat decrepit stone building which had a piece of cardboard at the door with the letters 'N.O.I.C.' written on it. These letters stand for Naval Officer in Charge, so my spirits rose a little. At least there was someone from the Navy here. I went inside and found the N.O.I.C., introduced myself, and enquired what living and office accommodation was available for my party. This query brought a loud guffaw in reply and the comment, 'Go outside and have a look at the place before you ask a question like that.' Somewhat despondently I concurred and went outside. I had not gone far before I realised that I was in an even worse position than when searching for accommodation in Calcutta. I had not only myself but also my party to consider. The 'base' consisted of a beach-head which had been occupied by the army, who were encamped in tents. There was only one stone building in the area and that was occupied by N.O.I.C. Other than that there were a few ramshackle palm-thatched huts. The task of setting up a D.E.M.S. base here seemed, at this point, a little daunting to say the least.

Having completed a quick tour of inspection of the area on foot, I returned to the jetty with the intention of bringing my party ashore. The boat was waiting for me at the jetty and I returned to the ship and had lunch. After lunch I briefed my Petty Officer on the situation ashore following my cursory inspection, and told him I would take him and the party ashore, leaving them there to carry out a more detailed reconnaissance while I visited some of the ships lying in the anchorage. Having dropped the Petty Officer and his party ashore, I then started visiting various ships in the anchorage, in course of which I came across a cargo vessel which was staying for a week or so awaiting orders, and had some spare passenger accommodation. I persuaded the captain to put me up temporarily in one of his spare cabins and also to feed me whilst on board. He was a little reluctant about the feeding part and wanted to be paid cash for this. I assured him that I would sign any vouchers for food, and that these would be paid if forwarded to Naval Headquarters in Calcutta. He finally agreed and thus my immediate accommodation problem was solved.

Returning ashore, I found that my party there had been making good progress. They had 'acquired' two army bell tents (I did not enquire how) and were in the process of erecting them.

One of these tents could be used as living quarters for the men and the other as an office. We were making headway in setting up a base! No furniture other than a couple of empty orange boxes, nor any feeding arrangements for the men but these would come. We were in business. In the course of searching for somewhere to 'set up shop' we had looked at some of the unused palm-thatched huts, but found them infested with all manner of 'creepy-crawlies' which was a little off-putting, especially for living quarters. I had not been in the country long enough to learn that there are two main kinds of creepy-crawlies; those that bite or sting or suck your blood (like ants, scorpions, or mosquitoes) and those which are harmless, like cockroaches, bats and lizards.

Now that we had set up shop I was able to start visiting the ships coming into the anchorage. I was beginning to enjoy the experience – or would have if it were not for the fact that the dysentery had not yet entirely left me. The food on my ship was good, and it was very pleasant, after a busy day inspecting ships and writing up reports, to come 'home', have a good dinner and sit on deck watching the sun go down over the Bay of Bengal. These sunsets are one of my abiding memories of Burma. In the evenings it is calm and the sea goes like glass. The setting sun is like a crimson ball dropping down, seemingly getting larger as it falls. One almost expects it to sizzle as it touches the sea and casts a path of fire from the horizon to the ship. As it slowly drops out of sight, both sky and sea are bathed in its after-glare, which imperceptibly changes colour from fiery red to purple to dark blue and finally to black as darkness falls. In the tropics darkness comes quickly after sunset.

A few days later, when considering that matters were well in hand and I was getting on with the job I had been sent to do, I could not help wondering what might happen next to shake me out of my complacency. I did not have long to wait to find out. After dinner one evening the captain of the ship I was staying on advised me he had received sailing orders and would be leaving the next day. Why was I continually bereft of somewhere to live since arriving in this part of the world? This particular problem was becoming tiresome. The next morning after breakfast, I took my leave of my erstwhile home, going ashore with all my baggage in the ship's boat for the last time. As I moved my belongings into my office (bell tent) I could not help wondering where I was going to sleep that night.

I was sitting in the office, wondering what to do next, and had just decided that I had better start visiting some of the ships in the anchorage to see if I could get a berth in any of them on a temporary basis, when in walked a Naval officer. He had just arrived in Chauk Pyu and informed me that he was the officer originally drafted here and whom I had temporally relieved because of his sickness. Having regained his full health he had come hot-foot down to Ramree Island to relieve me, with orders that I was to return to Calcutta immediately.

He could not have arrived at a more propitious moment. Once again, my immediate accommodation problem was unexpectedly solved by events. However, I was now presented with a new problem. How to get back to Calcutta? Because of the efforts being made to advance on Rangoon, all of the shipping was moving south, whereas I now wanted to go northwards to Calcutta. During my short time at Ramree Island I had noticed Royal Air Force planes quite frequently flying fairly low over the island. I presumed that there must be a landing place somewhere nearby. On enquiry I found that the army engineers had indeed constructed a landing strip on the island. I prevailed upon the driver of an army jeep to drive me to the airstrip, where I went to see the Flying Control Officer.

Arriving at the airstrip, which consisted of a length of metal meshing laid on a flat piece of ground, I noticed one or two DC-3 Dakota aircraft coming and going, and also one parked beside the strip. I spoke to the F.C.O. and enquired whether by any chance there were any planes going to Calcutta that I could cadge a lift on. He said, 'Yes, there's one leaving at 2.30 this afternoon.' Thereupon I hurriedly departed back to my office to collect my gear, returning to the airstrip just in time to scramble onto the Calcutta-bound freight plane before it departed.

This was 1945. Air travel was not a normal form of transport, even for service personnel in the armed forces, and I wondered whether I was breaking any rules. It was also my first time in an aeroplane. This was a cargo plane; there were no seats except for metal benches running the length of the plane, one on each side. No such luxury as a cushion. Along the floor, up the centre of the cabin, was a row of large packing cases, secured to the floor by steel wires. I figured that the plane must sometimes carry passengers, as there were seat belts at intervals along the bench seats. There was one other passenger besides myself: an Indian Army officer. The plane taxied to the end of the airstrip and after what seemed a very short, bumpy run, took off and we were airborne. Not having flown before, it was an interesting experience for me, and I sat beside one of the small windows to watch our progress.

For some miles the plane flew fairly low along the coastline. I could see both the land and the sea. The land was covered down to the shoreline with dense jungle, and it was like flying over a green carpet. With a cloudless sky above, the sea was a deep blue. The plane proceeded so smoothly there was very little sense of motion. I remember thinking, if this is air travel, I think I like it. After about an hour's travelling I was looking out of the window and noticed that the sea below had become very rough, with quite a lot of white water on the surface. Also, ahead of the plane was a large black cloud. The plane was also now climbing steeply, and we were soon flying at what I estimated to be several thousand feet above the ground.

Neither the other passenger nor myself had our seatbelts fastened, and the next thing I remember is being catapulted across the inside of the plane as it started some very violent movement; caused, I afterwards found out, by suddenly entering a tropical electrical storm. Apparently such storms were a frequent occurrence in the area. I have a vivid memory of the Indian Army officer and myself frantically staggering and clawing our way back around the packing cases to our seats, then struggling to secure ourselves into our seat belts. For about 20 minutes the plane flew through the storm and seemed to me to do everything but loop the loop.

I have flown many times since, in many different planes, but cannot remember such violent movement as on that first occasion. All the while the lightning was flashing all around the plane as it plunged and soared through the murk with its engines racing and slowing by turns. The violent movement was getting the better of the Indian officer, and the poor fellow became terribly ill with air sickness. There was little I could do to help him, strapped into my seat as I was, and afraid that if I undid my belt I would be quickly flung in all directions.

With extraordinary suddenness the plane flew out of the storm – as quickly as it had flown into it – and we were again flying along smoothly and serenely in a clear blue sky. That plane took a lot of punishment on that flight and forever afterwards I have always had a great respect for the old Dakota, which at the time was the workhorse of the air force. There were no further incidents on the flight, which ended by our landing at Dum Dum airport in Calcutta. The journey, which had taken a couple of days by ship, had been completed in a few hours by air.

Chapter 8

Calcutta

I lost no time getting myself from the airport to the D.E.M.S. office in Calcutta docks. During my absence in Burma the staff there had been working on my accommodation problem. I was introduced to Tony Chambers, who had been serving for some time in Calcutta as a D.E.M.S. Inspection Officer. He advised me that there was a spare bed in his digs which his landlord was willing to let me have if I wanted it. This seemed an excellent arrangement, as we would be working together and could travel together so I gladly accepted the offer. As matters turned out Tony and I got on extremely well together, and although we moved several times, we shared digs for the rest of my time in Calcutta.

Having satisfactorily solved my accommodation problem, I could now settle down to the routine of living and working in this tropical city. Tony was invaluable in 'showing me the ropes' and I was soon settled into the quite different routine of life in India. Local traditions in India are completely different from European countries and take a little getting used to. The first thing I found was that one has to have a whole staff of servants. Firstly, one must have a 'boy'. He is one's personal servant or valet and supervises any other servants. He looks after one's clothes, waits at table, etc. Then there has to be a cook to look after the food and a sweeper who is responsible for keeping the place clean. In the case of a family with children, an ayah or nursemaid is needed. The predominant religion in India is Hinduism and the caste system is very much in evidence. For example, the 'boy' is higher caste than the sweeper. If the boy is waiting at table and drops something on the floor, he cannot stoop to pick it up or he would break his caste; he must therefore summon the sweeper to pick it up. Everyone has their own personal boy, but other servants such as cook or sweeper can be shared. Thus, Tony and I each had our own 'boys' but shared cook and sweeper with the other occupants of the house.

Securing the services of a good boy was not easy. The main difficulty was to find someone who was trustworthy and honest; someone who would not steal your cigarettes and drink or use your clothes. Petty theft was a recurring problem. We fired many for having 'sticky fingers'. One case in particular comes to mind. This individual made a habit of having a regular tipple from our gin bottle. We kept our drink in the bottom of a wardrobe in the bedroom. At one stage we thought the level in the gin bottle was going down quicker than it should, so we set a trap. Tony and

I agreed that neither of us would touch that particular gin bottle after the level had gone about three quarters down, where we marked it. Sure enough, we found that the level continued to go down about an inch each day. We decided to stop it. We poured about half a pint of ammonia into the bottle. The following day the level was down another inch but it never went any further!

On another occasion I found that my boy was wearing my clothes. We wore tropical uniform, which consisted of shorts and a white shirt with shoulder tabs on which were tied our badges of rank. Because the weather was so hot and humid we had to change our clothes three or four times a day. The drill was to come in at, say, 11 o'clock in the morning and change into fresh clothes after showering. The old clothes, which after a morning's work in the docks since six o'clock would be soaked in perspiration, would be thrown into the dhobi box for washing after removing the rank badges. It was part of the boy's job to collect these soiled clothes and take them regularly to the 'dhobi wallah' (launderer) to be washed and then returned to my wardrobe. Dinner in the evenings was always a fairly formal affair, for which one had to dress properly. Our dress was Naval 'number sevens', which consisted of long white trousers with a white long-sleeved tunic buttoned up to the neck. The boys waiting at the table were expected to wear their best clothes.

One evening while having dinner, I thought the clothes my boy was wearing looked familiar. I kept an eye on him as he came to place a plate in front of me, and was horrified to find that he was wearing my white shirt and shorts, which I had discarded earlier in the day when changing. He was getting a 'turn' out of my clothes before sending them to the wash! I did not make any comment during the meal, but the following morning his employment with me came to an abrupt end.

These two incidents were not isolated; indeed they were typical of the problems everyone had with servants, and one became used to it in the end. There were always stories going around about such problems. One such tale concerned a servant who had been sacked for some such misdemeanour and had the audacity to ask for a reference to take to his next employer. His erstwhile employer wrote the following reference: 'This man has done me well. If he does you as well as he has done me, you will be well and truly done.' With his limited knowledge of the intricacies of the English language, the errant servant went off thinking he had an excellent reference.

The climate in Calcutta is enervating until one becomes acclimatised. The temperature averaged around 104 degrees Fahrenheit in the shade. Because the city is in the middle of the Ganges delta and there is so much water around, the humidity is in the high eighties. It was so hot down in the docks where we worked, one could not stand in one place for more than a few moments, as the hot concrete burned one's feet through the leather soles of one's shoes. In order to work in the coolest part of the day we started at six o'clock in the morning and finished at midday. After that it was simply too hot to work. It is said that with practice one can get used to anything. After a while I became used to the conditions and thought nothing of it. Our whole daily routine was built up around our work day of six to twelve.

Each morning Tony and I would drive from our digs to the office in the service vehicle which had been allocated to us for our transport. This was a heavy-duty four-wheel-drive station wagon which seated about six people but also doubled up as a goods carrier for transporting naval stores, etc. It had fairly large wheels, which meant that the floor of the vehicle was about two feet or more above road level. This was useful when driving over rough jungle tracks or even around the city during the monsoon when flash floods often meant driving through a couple of feet of water.

Jottings of a Young Sailor

Our first job on arriving at the office was to read through the Admiralty signals reporting shipping movements all over the world, to see what ships were on their way to Calcutta and when they would arrive. This would tell us what ships to expect in port each day. We would then contact the harbour master to see where in the port the ships were going to dock. Some would enter various docks off the river, while others would moor in the river at mooring buoys. Oil tankers moored at a specially constructed oil jetty at a place called Budge Budge, about 10 miles down river from the city. Thus we planned our work for the morning before leaving the office to visit the ships.

Calcutta, at the time, was a very busy port. Every ship arriving had to be visited. There were half a dozen Inspection Officers, of which I was one, and it was hard enough work getting round all the ships before they left. Climbing up and down 30- to 40-foot gangways in the hot sun to board the ships was not particularly pleasant. Working in the docks day after day, we became used to the heat and humidity but we felt sorry for the ships' crews. I would often make my way up to the Captain's cabin on the bridge of a ship to find the captain sitting, gasping and mopping his brow and enquiring how on earth I could work in such conditions. He had just come from the open ocean where the fast passage of the ship caused a cooling breeze. Now he was a hundred miles up river from the sea, stationary, with no chance of getting cool until he returned to sea.

Visiting the ships moored in the river presented special problems. The river Hoogly which flows through Calcutta is fast-flowing and deep. The only way to board the ships was to go down to the riverside and hire a sampan. This is a small native boat, a sort of cross between a canoe and a rowing boat, which is propelled by a large oar over the stern worked by the single boatman. I would get the boatman to take me out to the ship, perhaps a hundred yards or so from the river bank, and ask him to wait for me. I could usually complete my business on the ship in about half an hour. On some occasions I might be delayed, and on return to the ship's side would find the sampan gone, leaving me marooned on the ship with no way of getting ashore. Then I would have to start waving and shouting to other sampans along the riverbank to try to attract their attention and persuade them to come out to rescue me. There was a reason why these boatmen did not like going out to the moored ships.

Ships moored in the river were moored by heavy chains ahead and astern to mooring buoys in two rows about 10 or 15 yards apart. Each ship was about one ship's length ahead of the one astern. It all looked so secure and satisfactory, but the Hoogly is a tidal river which has a 'bore' which arrives after high tide twice a day. This bore is caused by the incoming tide being forced up the ever-narrowing channels of the delta. By the time it reaches Calcutta, 100 miles up river from the sea, it has built up to a wall of water four or five feet high. This fast-flowing wave meets the equally fast outward flow of the river, resulting in a maelstrom of swirling water. This would pull the ships moored in the river in all directions at once for a period of five minutes or so until the bore passed and all became quiet again. While the bore was passing the moorings there was a lot of ominous grinding of metal as the heavy ships pulled at their mooring cables first in one direction and then in another. I was once caught out in a sampan amongst the moorings when the bore arrived, and it is not a pleasant experience. I don't know who was more scared, myself or the boatman rowing the sampan.

Visiting oil tankers involved driving 10 miles or so down a jungle road to the oil jetty at Budge Budge. On one occasion the only vehicle I could obtain was an old Ford 15-hundredweight truck. Unknown to me at the time, a young Sub Lieutenant had taken it out on a spree the night before and crashed it into a wall. The only apparent damage was a bent fender; what was not apparent was the cracked radiator which allowed the cooling water to drain slowly from the engine. When I was eight miles or so into the jungle I smelled burning and saw smoke coming from under the bonnet. I stopped and opened the bonnet, to be met with a cloud of smoke and a dull red glow coming from the direction of the engine block. Although the engine had not seized, it was obvious I could not go any further. I was marooned in the middle of the jungle, miles from anywhere. In those days there were no such things as mobile phones and I did not have a radio in the vehicle, so I had no means of communication.

Something of a predicament. My only hope was to try to make some sort of temporary repair to enable me to drive the vehicle back to Calcutta. I could not even get near the engine until it cooled down, and cooling it was not easy when the air temperature was more than a hundred degrees Fahrenheit. I opened the bonnet on both sides to let as much air as possible into the engine, then sat in the driver's seat waiting patiently for things to cool down a bit. It was not long before a gang of small Indian boys arrived from some nearby jungle village and started jumping around me excitedly, wanting to know what was wrong.

Having explained my problem as best I could, using a mixture of my limited knowledge of Hindustani, some English and a lot of sign language, they then descended upon my red hot engine with youthful enthusiasm, determined to cool it down by fanning it with banana and other such large leaves. It was as much as I could do to prevent them from burning their hands on the flaming hot metal of the engine. I then got the idea that we might aid the cooling process by sprinkling water on the hot metal. This had to be done very gently at first, otherwise there was a good chance the block would crack if it was cooled too quickly. There was plenty of water around, as I was in the middle of a swamp; but what to carry it in? I had no tin or other receptacle.

My young helpers soon solved that problem. Living in the jungle, they were very adept at folding plant leaves into containers of all sizes, and I soon had a constant supply of water being carried in these home-made jugs from nearby ponds. At first I had some difficulty restraining them from dousing the hot engine with gallons of water. The loud spluttering and hissing and clouds of steam caused by the first few drops of water added to their excitement. It was a slow process but I was determined not to crack the block by too rapid cooling, as this would have meant abandoning the vehicle. After about half an hour or so the metal was cool enough for us to apply the water more liberally, and from then it was not long before the engine was down to normal temperature. I filled the radiator, checked there was no damage to the fuel line and ignition leads, pulled the starter cord and – lo and behold! – the engine started. I could not believe it. I gained a lot of respect for the reliability of those Ford engines. My young helpers were as delighted with the outcome as I was and started whooping and cheering when the engine started.

Our frenzied repair efforts in the hot sun had made us thirsty. One of the boys scaled a nearby coconut palm with the ease of a monkey and cut down a couple of coconuts. One of the older boys had a kukri, which is a large curved knife used for many purposes in India and by the Gurkha soldiers for fighting. With the knife he deftly cut a number of slashes in the husk, which made a perfect lip for drinking the coconut milk. The milk is cool, has a pleasant taste and is very refreshing. It is also the only safe thing to drink. There is a lot of water around, but it is contaminated and unfit to drink. Having refreshed ourselves with the cool coconut milk, I gave each of my young helpers a few Annas (small Indian coins), got into the truck and drove slowly back to the office in Calcutta without further incident. There I lost no time in contacting the young officer who had damaged the truck, pointing out to him the error of his ways.

Service vehicles which were damaged or unserviceable for any reason were supposed to be taken out of service immediately until repaired, and not left lying around for some unsuspecting person to drive off into potentially dangerous situations.

When we stopped work in the docks round about midday, we drove back to our digs, had a bath and flopped down on our beds for the afternoon siesta. At this time of day it was too hot outside to do anything. Everyone else was doing the same. There was very little movement of people outside. Even the Indian cart drivers with their water buffalo carts watered their animals. These buffalo carts were a common sight in the city. The large, heavy carts were drawn by two water buffalo, which are quite large animals, larger and heavier than most horses, and there are few if any horses in India anyway. There was a local law which compelled cart drivers to water their beasts so many times a day to stop their skins drying out. It was a common sight in the city to see a driver stopped beside a fire hydrant watering his animals. He turned the hydrant on full and put his bare foot on it so that the water squirted in a spray over the animals, who obviously very much enjoyed the treatment.

The afternoon heat was not conducive to sleep, so we mostly lay on our beds and read books, chatted or just watched the antics of the lizards which populated the walls of the bedroom. The walls of all of the rooms had their resident lizards, maybe two or three in every room. We welcomed their presence. They were clean and they fed on the various insects which were always invading the house through the open windows. It was fascinating to watch them. If a fly landed on the wall six feet away from a lizard, it would start moving towards it so slowly the movement would be imperceptible. When a foot away it would stop for a few seconds, then, in a movement so fast it could not be seen, the fly was gone, to be replaced by the lizard on the same spot. They could move incredibly quickly and could jump as well. I once watched a lizard stalking a fly into an alcove in the room where a wardrobe stood, with a space of about nine inches between it and the adjoining wall. The lizard followed the fly round the corner of the wall into the alcove. When the fly took off from the wall and landed on the side of the wardrobe, the lizard jumped the nine-inch gap and the fly was gone. An amazing piece of acrobatics. One day Tony decided to try to catch one of the lizards. It was low down on the wall, stalking a fly. Tony started slowly stalking the lizard. To my surprise he got near enough to catch hold of the lizard's tail. What surprised me more was that the lizard merely ran away, leaving his tail in Tony's hand. Apparently this is quite normal and the lizard grows a new tail.

Round about four-thirty or five in the afternoon the heat starts to ease slightly and it is Tiffin time, or time for afternoon tea. Everyone rises from their siesta, has a bath, puts on clean clothes and is ready for the afternoon activities. Tony and I both belonged to several clubs in the city. Temporary honorary membership was granted to serving officers of the British forces. In the afternoons we might go for a swim at the swimming club. This club had large premises in a city centre park, with an indoor pool and a large outdoor pool with adjoining restaurant and bar. It was a very pleasant place to spend a leisurely afternoon, where one could jump into the water occasionally to cool off. The coolest pool was the indoor one, which was shaded from the sun. The sun shining on the outdoor pool sometimes made the water unpleasantly hot; this was remedied by the pool staff dumping in large blocks of ice which they obtained from the local ice factory. When this happened, people in the pool amused themselves by swimming to the floating ice blocks and trying to climb on to them to cool off. It never took long for the ice to melt, but it did have the desired effect of cooling the water for a while.

Another club we frequented had tennis courts. We often went there for a game in the afternoons. We played quite a lot, because the courts were floodlit at night so that we could play in the evenings after dinner as well. In fact we played more often after dinner, as it was very tiring playing out in the afternoon sun, when the temperature in the shade was over 100° F. We spent a lot of our evenings at this club, as besides the tennis courts there was a billiards table and a piano in the same room. A young Sub Lieutenant (the one who had crashed the truck) often joined us in the evenings. He was an accomplished pianist. He had competed his L.R.A.M. (Licentiate of the Royal Academy of Music) exams at an early age. He would sit at the piano in the billiard room and play non-stop all night. He could play classical music, such as Mozart, Chopin, Strauss or whatever, but he preferred, of all things, 'boogie-woogie' music, which was all the rage at the time. One would ask him to play a bit of, say, Beethoven. He would be in the middle of a beautiful rendering of the Moonlight Sonata, get fed up with it and suddenly burst into boogie-woogie. It was fascinating to watch him improvising for hours on the keyboard. He didn't even stop to have a drink. We would put a pint of beer on top of the piano for him and he would work his way through this by lifting the glass occasionally with one hand and drinking while continuing to play with the other.

One night we were playing tennis at the club by floodlight. There was a bang and all the lights went out, leaving us in complete darkness. We went into the clubhouse and smelled burning and found the entrance hall on fire. We called the fire service, but by the time they arrived we had managed to beat the fire out ourselves. The fire had started in the electrical distribution box in the entrance hall, apparently by a large cockroach walking across two electrical contacts!

Some afternoons we spent shopping and looking around the bazaars in the market area. An expedition into the Calcutta traffic by car is an experience in itself. I have never seen anywhere else such a dense concentration of so many modes of transport as in Calcutta. At a city centre intersection, when the traffic lights turn red, the traffic builds up. A cart drawn by two enormous water buffalo lumbers to a stop, followed by a bus crowded with passengers, not only filling all the seats but also standing on the bumpers and sitting on the roof and bonnet. Around the bus creep the cars, filling every available space. Then come the motor bikes, mopeds and bicycles, of which there seem to be hundreds (Calcutta is a flat city with no hills and is ideal for cyclists). Waiting for the lights to change, the cyclists worm their way in front of all the four-wheeled traffic. Finally the rickshaws (one-man-powered version) wheedle their way in front of everything else. The rickshaw wallahs wear a small bell tied to their third finger with a piece of string, which they use as a warning of their presence by tapping on the shaft of the rickshaw as they pull it along.

During the 1940s, when I was in the city, electric horns on cars in Calcutta were banned because it was found that all drivers drove with their hands on the horn all the time, thus making their use quite ineffective. As a consequence of this ban, all cars and lorries were fitted with the old fashioned type of horn which was sounded by squeezing a rubber bulb. When the lights turned green the scene was extraordinary. In a cacophony of sound caused by the loud and continuous honk-honks of the many motor horns, joined by numerous bicycle bells and the urgent clink-clink of the rickshaw bells and shouts of the cart drivers urging their lethargic buffalo into motion, the whole mass of transport moves off like the start of a marathon race. Because all the slowest moving vehicles are inevitably at the front, it takes about half a mile to sort itself out, by which time the next traffic lights have come up and the whole process starts over again.

Add to this conglomeration of traffic thousands of pedestrians of all kinds, milling around and spilling onto the roads and the street hawkers, snake charmers, etc. lining the edge of the road, to say nothing of the odd troupe of monkeys who gallop down the road with gay abandon, and one has an idea of what the centre of the city looks like normally. I have mentioned before the enormous loads which porters carry on their heads. I was once astonished to see in a city centre street six men carrying a grand piano, upside down, on their heads! They were evenly spaced around the edge of the upturned piano, all walking in step and keeping up a fairly brisk pace as they wended their way through the pedestrians and other traffic. I often wondered how they got the piano up onto their heads and how they got it down again when they reached their destination.

In Chowringhee, which is the main street in the city centre, there were many very good shops – such as the Army and Navy Stores – comparable with the large department stores in European cities. Also jewellers, tailors, furniture stores, etc. However, the most interesting place to shop was in the market or bazaar in the back streets. Here one could buy anything from a pin to a wheelbarrow. After living in the city for some time, one got to know where to go for the best bargains and best quality goods. There were excellent tailors where I used to obtain my tailor-made tropical uniforms. Silversmiths, goldsmiths, Benares brass merchants, wood carvers and all manner of craft works. The Indians are masters of craftwork. For example, in the silver shops there was a bewildering array of silver filigree jewellery and ornaments. The same next door in the shops which sold nothing but gold items. Next to that would be a shop full to the ceiling with nothing but Benares brass, from small ashtrays to huge ornaments. Each shop had its own speciality.

Then there was the fruit market, with its unique smell of fresh fruit mixed with the scents of flowers and spices. A colourful scene with rows of all kinds of tropical fruits stacked in neat pyramids. Apples, oranges, bananas, mangos, lychees, lemons etc. Further along were similar rows of stalls with stacked pyramids of innumerable varieties of nuts. Walnuts, brazils, chestnuts, cobnuts, and many more unrecognisable varieties. We frequently bought bags of different kinds of nuts as they were always fresh and made delicious eating. I often wondered how so many varieties of nuts from different parts of the world were so easily available but they were always there and always fresh.

I once entered a shop specialising in fine timber furniture, some of which was beautifully inlaid with ivory and ebony. I caught sight of a large pyramid of round tables of different sizes piled one on top of the other. Each table was identical in design. The top was beautifully inlaid in a design depicting the Taj Mahal. Each of the three legs were carved into the shape of an elephant's head complete with ivory tusks. I suppose there were a dozen or more of the tables in the pyramid, ranging in size from about five feet across down to a tiny one on top measuring six inches in diameter. I thought I must buy one of these, but which one? Very difficult to decide which would be the most appropriate size to fit in one's house back home. In the end I decided on one which had a top about eighteen inches across which would serve as a coffee table. I also had to consider the question of how I was going to get it home to the U.K.

My friend Tony had married shortly before coming to India and was trying to furnish a new house. One day he was in the bazaar looking for carpets and I followed him into a carpet shop. Here one could buy good quality Indian carpets ridiculously cheap in comparison with prices at home. While I was waiting for Tony to select three or four carpets, which he was going to have shipped home, my eye fell on a beautiful large carpet hanging up on display. It had a plain cream ground with a pattern of large bunches of roses in each corner and a large circular pattern of roses in the centre. The stems and flowers of the roses were raised above the level of the background, giving an embossed effect. I enquired about the carpet and was told that it was one of a pair specially made for some Indian potentate who had them designed specially. Apparently he could not decide which design he liked most, so the factory had carpets made up to both designs to enable him to see the finished product. The carpet I was looking at was the one he did not take. I was so taken with the carpet I decided to buy it. It cost £50 sterling, which was quite a high price for a carpet in 1945. Tony thought I was mad. He had just bought four carpets for the same price. However, I knew that the quality of the one I bought was such that it would last for many years, and I was happy with my purchase.

During my time in Calcutta I purchased many items in the bazaar. Here it was so unlike shopping at home, where everything was scarce with the austerity of war. Not only was food in short supply but luxury goods such as jewellery and novelty goods were practically unobtainable. In the shops and bazaars here there was an abundance of food and all kinds of luxury goods and souvenirs. I ended up with quite a store of items I wanted to send home. Normally at that time, it was virtually impossible to get anything home from India unless one brought it oneself. The postal service was useless, as anything of any value was inevitably stolen long before it left the country.

Luckily Tony and I had a reliable means of sending parcels home, arising from the work we were doing at the time. Because we were part of an organisation which was servicing merchant ships on a world-wide basis, we had access to the somewhat secret information giving the movements of all Allied merchant shipping all over the world. If we had something we wanted to send home, we parcelled it up, addressed it clearly and placed the appropriate English postage stamps on it (the stamps we were able to obtain through official channels). We then looked through the Admiralty signals to find a ship which would shortly come into Calcutta on its way home to the United Kingdom. When the ship arrived in Calcutta we would visit it in the normal course of our work and ask the Captain if he would mind posting a parcel for us when he reached his first English port. We would give him a list of items contained in the parcel to satisfy the curiosity of any customs officials, and usually the Captain was only too willing to oblige, as for our part we had provided him with our best service whilst in our port in relation to his ship's armament and gunnery personnel.

When the ship left Calcutta we were able, through our daily incoming signals in the office, to trace its progress home, perhaps via Madras, Bombay, Suez, Gibraltar and Liverpool. When the ship reached Liverpool I would write home and advise my parents that a parcel would probably reach them in a couple of days. Unlike parcel post, letter post from India was quite fast and reliable at the time.

As regards the carpet I purchased, this was too large an item for parcel post. The shop where I purchased it arranged to have it shipped to my home address, and also paid for the shipping. They were able to obtain for me the name of the ship carrying the carpet, so that I was able to trace the passage of this ship all the way home. There was however a problem. I traced passage of the ship as far as Port Said at the Mediterranean end of the Suez canal, and then I lost it completely. It just disappeared from any of the ship movement signals. What had happened to it? If it had been earlier in the war I would have suspected the ship might have been torpedoed, as the Mediterranean was an extremely dangerous place then but this was near the end of the war in Europe and there was no longer such danger there.

Jottings of a Young Sailor

After frantically sending a number of signals enquiring from several sources the whereabouts of the ship, I discovered that she had had a mishap after leaving Port Said. Apparently when half way along the Mediterranean, the propeller fell off! More frantic signals elicited the fact that the ship had been towed into Taranto in Italy and that a new propeller would have to be shipped out from England to effect a repair. Every week I impatiently checked the signals to see if there was any sign of movement. It was many months before the new propeller was shipped out, and many more before the repair was made. In the event, by the time the ship was repaired, set sail again for home and arrived in Liverpool, the war had ended and I was on the way home myself. I arrived home one day after the carpet! It had not yet been opened from its packing. I unpacked the carpet myself, something I certainly had not expected to do when I dispatched it from India.

Chapter 9

Mynah Birds and Monkeys

During much of my time in Calcutta, both Tony and I were living in the homes of British expatriates as part of the family. We lived for some time in the home of Colin Prescott and his wife. Colin was the Chief Mechanical Engineer of the Bengal and Assam Railway, one of the large railway companies in India. The Prescotts' two sons were army officers and had, with their wives and children, been Japanese prisoners of war since the fall of Singapore early in the far eastern war. The house was a large and comfortable one in the Railway executives' housing compound, which was like a housing estate enclosed by a surrounding wall and containing gardens, tennis courts and a swimming pool for the residents. The compound was situated on the outskirts of Calcutta, next door to the much larger compound enclosing the palace of the Viceroy of India.

When the Japanese war ended we had to leave this comfortable home, as the rooms we were occupying were required for preparation for the Prescotts' returning sons and their families.

We were fortunate in being able to take up residence with another family. This time it was with a Hoogly river Pilot and his wife and baby daughter. Although not as salubrious as our previous home, it was with a seafaring family with whom we had many things in common and we had many happy times in their household.

These two households, together with some of the other places in which I temporarily lodged, all had one thing in common. Like many other households in India they had a resident mynah bird. People in India have mynah birds as pets like people in Britain have cats and dogs. In appearance the mynah bird is something like a large blackbird; not particularly attractive but it has one great attribute. It is a natural mimic, much more so than parrots or cockatoos. It mimics other birds, animals and humans with amazing accuracy. So much so that, in the case of humans, one can recognise the person being imitated.

These birds are usually kept in large cages like a parrot cage. Colin Prescott had a mynah in a cage hanging in the hall of his house at the bottom of the stairs Every morning, when anyone came down the stairs, the mynah would say 'Good morning' in a loud voice and insist on being answered. If you chose to ignore the bird as you walked past its cage, you were followed into the dining room with a 'Good morning, good morning, good morning, good morning!' repeated with an increasing crescendo of sound. One soon became used to replying with a cheery 'Good morning'. When I first went to the house it struck me as slightly odd the way everyone casually said 'Good morning' to the bird as they passed by in the mornings. In another house in which I stayed there was a young baby which occasionally burst into a fit of crying. The mynah had picked up the young mother's response of 'What are you crying for?' with the result that every time the baby cried and before the mother could say anything the mynah called out, 'What are you crying for?' The extraordinary thing was that the baby frequently responded to this call by stopping crying. These birds eavesdropped on conversations, and if one was within earshot one had to be careful what one was saying, as you never knew when something you said was going to be repeated, perhaps quite out of context, at a later time. For example if you dropped a hammer on your toe and said 'Oh bother!' (or words to that effect) your expletive might well be repeated later by the bird if a door slammed or someone dropped a plate in the kitchen.

Mynah birds were certainly very entertaining and could be very amusing. Some of them could build up quite a large vocabulary, and it was nearly possible to have a conversation of sorts with them.

Tony and I had for some time given up sleeping under mosquito nets. For one thing we found they were a mixed blessing. Sleeping under one in the humid heat, it was even more difficult to keep cool. Also it was all very well sealing the net all round under the mattress, but one had to get in there; and when climbing in, a mosquito could get in unnoticed at the same time. Then he was sealed in there with you and able to feed on you all night. Another problem was when driving to the office in the morning. The station wagon we used for transport was the type of vehicle which had the engine between the two front seats. When we parked the vehicle outside our house at night, the engine casing would be warm and would attract a swarm of mosquitoes to nest around it for the night. When Tony and I sat in the two front seats in the morning and started the engine, we soon found the bare knees sticking out of our shorts covered with bites from the disturbed mosquitoes. We gave up using mosquito nets over our beds at night.

It was only a matter of time before one was bitten by the wrong mosquito. One morning I awoke with severe head pains and a temperature. I told Tony to tell the office I would not be in for work. He said he would check back with me at lunchtime. By the time he returned at lunchtime I felt worse, so a doctor was called. He examined me and informed me I had Dengue fever. An ambulance was called and I was carted off to the local military hospital, where I spent a most uncomfortable few weeks trying to get rid of my affliction. All I can remember of my tine there is of the seeming lack of any form of treatment other than starving. I was not allowed anything to eat until the last few days before leaving. For the first week or so I did not want to eat, but was encouraged to drink gallons of fresh lime juice and was left literally to sweat it out. After a fortnight with nothing to eat, by which time the fever was beginning to ease, I was feeling hungry but despite my urgent requests for food I was not allowed any. I was reduced to asking my visiting friends to smuggle in bars of chocolate which I scoffed at night when no one was watching!

One strange incident in hospital remains etched in my memory. The time had finally arrived when I was allowed some food, but I was somewhat disappointed to find that all I was going to get was one pint of milk a day. This was set on my bedside locker each morning and I was required to have taken it all by evening. I don't like milk and never have, so I let it be known to the hospital staff that as far as I was concerned this was medicine and not food. I suggested that according to the advertisements, 'Guinness is good for you' and could I not have a pint of Guinness instead of a pint of milk. However, my suggestion was not given serious consideration and I dutifully continued taking my pint of milk each day.

One day, an extraordinary thing happened. As usual the pint of milk was placed on my bedside locker by a hospital orderly. I was still feeling very weak from the fever and just lay there on the bed. I remember looking at the glass full of milk and as I looked it suddenly, with a crack, spontaneously shattered into a thousand pieces. It was like some sort of conjuring trick where the glass was there one minute and was then gone in a flash. The milk did not disappear but just collapsed and poured all over the table top onto the floor. I had heard of glasses spontaneously shattering and was a bit sceptical about it, but not any more. I believe it may have something to do with the annealing of the glass making it susceptible to shattering. The noise and commotion amongst the other patients in the ward soon brought in some of the hospital staff, who demanded from me an explanation as to why the milk was all over the floor and where was the glass. When I recounted what had happened I was just not believed and was blamed for somehow having knocked the glass over. A new pint of milk appeared and I was told to drink it quickly before any more weird 'accidents' happened.

The 8th May 1945 arrived and it was a memorable day. For the first time for some weeks I was beginning to feel a bit better. I had recovered from the fever sufficiently to get out of bed for a short time each day, although I was still not allowed out of the hospital ward. While I was out of bed this day, I remember hearing a lot of cheering coming from outside the ward. Some of my fellow patients went out onto the landing. Some quickly came back and called the rest of us out. I went out to the landing to find someone on the landing below had a radio on and there was the voice of a B.B.C. commentator describing the scene of celebration in Trafalgar Square in London. 'The war has ended!' he was shouting. It was V.E. day and the war in Europe had just finished. The patients in the hospital received this piece of news with mixed feelings. After six long, hard years the war in Europe had at last been won. Great; but to us, in hospital in India, the jubilation seemed a bit premature. Our lads were still being slaughtered by the Japanese in the jungles of Burma not far away, and there was no sign of the war at sea or on land in the East coming to an end. As far as we were concerned it was 'business as usual' and there was no change in our daily war effort.

Another week passed and I had now recovered sufficiently to feel the urge to get out of hospital and back to work. When my doctor found out what kind of work I was doing, climbing up and down onto ships in the docks, he would not hear of me leaving unless I could be put on light duties. The D.E.M.S. Staff Officer who was my Commanding Officer gave the necessary assurance that I would only be required to do light office duties and I was released from hospital.

I found myself back in the D.E.M.S. office in Calcutta docks. It seemed strange after some weeks' absence. I was glad to be back but was feeling quite weak and doddery after my bout of fever, which had left me a stone lighter than before. One of the characteristics of Dengue is that it often leaves behind a wearisome feeling of depression which can take some time to shake off. The staff in the office were most sympathetic and all did their best to help me to rehabilitate myself into some sort of working routine.

With the end of the war in Europe, I had not been back in the office long before I received a letter from the manager of the insurance company where I had worked before joining the Navy, pointing out that the war was over and asking when I was likely to return to work in the company. Nothing was further from my mind. I had just come out of hospital and wanted to get back on my feet to continue the job I was doing in Calcutta. I wrote back rather curtly stating that the war in Europe might be over, but there was still very much a war on where I was and I had no idea when I would be free to return to the company.

The Far East war, although showing no signs of ending, was in fact in its final stages. The Ministry of War in London had issued details of qualifying service for the various war medals and campaign stars to be issued to serving members of the forces. We had just received these details at D.E.M.S. Calcutta and I was given the job of reading through and interpreting the instructions and getting them applied to all of the D.E.M.S. personnel in our area of operation. Although this was a desk job in the office, I was quite happy to take it on as there was no doubt that I was, at the time, physically incapable of doing anything more strenuous. It was interesting enough. I spent all day interviewing D.E.M.S. personnel passing through our barracks, ascertaining where they had served since joining the Navy, deciding which medals and campaign stars they were entitled to and recording this officially in their pay books. Working in the office was different from working around the ships in the docks. Different problems arose. One rather odd problem was the monkeys.

The D.E.M.S. offices were situated on one of the main roads out of the city, near the river. There were lots of trees around our compound and overhanging the office building. These trees were frequently occupied by families of monkeys, making a lot of noise with their chattering and squabbling. Because there was no glass in the windows and the shutters were left permanently open for ventilation, the monkeys often invaded our offices. They had absolutely no fear of humans and could move extraordinarily quickly if chased, so that we were never able to catch up with them. Even if one did, it was not wise to get too close as they could inflict a very bad bite. On more than one occasion I walked into my office to find a monkey sitting at my desk playing with the pencils. They became very adept at using pencils and would scribble gleefully on any piece of paper they could find, regardless of the fact that it may be an important file. Another annoying habit was their propensity to use office objects such as rulers, pencils, paper weights etc. as missiles to throw at one another when playing. The monkeys travelled around in families, the very young ones clinging round their mothers' necks while moving. If a family playing in the trees outside decided to come in through an open window, they created havoc in the office before being driven out.

My work at this time was not physically demanding, but had some therapeutic effect as it exercised the mind. At the same time, while off duty, I started physical exercise by a daily swim in the pool and an occasional game of tennis. It was not long before I shrugged off the last vestiges of the depression, regained some of my lost weight and was feeling a bit more like my old self. I suggested to the D.E.M.S. Staff Officer that it was time I went back to my old job as an Inspection Officer and he readily agreed. It was something of a relief to get back to work on the ships after what seemed like an endless time trying to get rid of the effects of the Dengue.

Around this time there were some staff movements. The Senior Inspection Officer was transferred elsewhere and my friend Tony, who had up to now been doing the same job in the docks as myself, was promoted to replace him. In typical naval fashion he was neither promoted in rank or pay, despite having more responsibility. Not long after this, an event occurred which had far-reaching effects and altered the whole course of the war. On 6th August 1945 the first atom bomb was dropped on Hiroshima. There had for some time been rumours of the Allies' production of some sort of super weapon, so it was not altogether a surprise when news broke about the Hiroshima bombing. Our first reaction to the news was 'Great, maybe this will end the war', but no, nothing happened and it was not until another bomb was dropped on Nagasaki that the Japanese at last sued for peace. This was indeed good news. The war which had gone on for six long years was finally over. We could not believe it.

As expected, the ending of the war had a profound effect on the work we were doing. All of a sudden, instead of concentrating our efforts on the arming of ships and the maintenance of those arms, our role was reversed and we started disarming the same ships. For six years the main thrust had been fighting a war in many different parts of the world. Now the main object was to get the bulk of the armed forces home and demobilised. In D.E.M.S. we had many thousands of personnel on merchant ships all over the world, and they could not be sent home until the armament supplies on their ships had been removed. For ourselves in Calcutta, we seemed to be as busy as ever, removing arms from ships so that the men presently looking after them could be sent back to the U.K. We soon became even more hard-pressed. Signals were now coming through ever more frequently, calling for staff members to return to the U.K. for demobilisation. It was not long before Tony received his call to return to England for discharge. As it happened there was a merchant ship in the docks which we knew was bound for Liverpool. Tony lost no time arranging with the Captain to give him a berth on the passage home.

On Tony's departure I was promoted to replace him. Only my title was changed – to Chief Disarming Officer – and like Tony, I had no change in my rank or pay. I did have more work to do, because although I moved up to replace Tony, no one came to replace me. Six months later, in June 1946, my Order for Release arrived from the Admiralty in London. I received this with mixed feelings. On the one hand there was a great feeling of relief that the war was at last over, but on the other a feeling of regret that I would be leaving a way of life in the Navy which I had become used to and rather liked. Shortly after my release order arrived, we heard that the Senior Disarming Officer in Bangkok was leaving to return home. A replacement for him was urgently required. I was very tempted to apply for this job, as I had never been to Bangkok and would have liked to visit that part of the world. However, I decided against it because the job would last only six months, after which I would have to return to the U.K. This would mean my arriving home in the middle of winter, a prospect I did not relish after having spent a couple of years in the tropics. I therefore opted to return home immediately, arriving during summer in order to reduce as much as possible the effects of the change of climate.

Chapter 10

Home Again

Having opted to return to the U.K. immediately for demobilisation, I now had to find some means of transport to get me there. My preferred means would be to await the arrival in Calcutta of a merchant ship bound for the U.K. and negotiate a passage home with the Captain. However, such ships were few and far between. Actually, one had left Calcutta about a week previously, and I did not know when the next one would arrive. That ship was going home via Madras and Bombay, and I figured that if I caught the Bombay express train without delay

I might reach Bombay before the ship did. It was a gamble and a race against time, but it was worth taking. I rushed down to the local military hospital to get the usual batch of injections necessary before leaving, said a few hurried goodbyes, and caught the next Bombay express from Howrah station in Calcutta.

Unfortunately my gamble did not pay off. After the two and a half days' journey from Calcutta, I arrived in Bombay a few hours after the ship I had been chasing had sailed. This was a disappointment and because I was no longer in a position to see the international naval signals, I could not tell when another such ship would arrive in Bombay. I was now completely at the mercy of the military transport authorities for my transport to the U.K., a fact that I was to rue before very long.

I could not help noticing how my impressions of Bombay had changed since my first arrival there from the U.K. I vividly recall on disembarking from the ship on my first arrival the impact of the stifling heat and smell of the place. Now, having arrived after a stay in Calcutta, with its humid high temperatures of a hundred degrees Fahrenheit or more, I thought it a delightfully moderate climate with its refreshingly cool breeze coming in from the sea. On my first visit I could not get out of the place quickly enough. Now I was quite reluctant to leave.

Whilst speaking to the transport people I had expressed a wish to return to the U.K. in a merchant ship if possible, rather than in a large troopship. After a couple of days in the transit camp I was advised that an American 'Liberty' ship was in harbour and would shortly be leaving for home, and that I could take passage on her. I was quite happy with this as I had come across Liberty ships many times before and knew them as modern, fast merchant ships with a certain amount of passenger accommodation and well stocked with good food. However, I was in for not only another disappointment but something of a shock.

When I arrived on board I found that my merchant ship had been converted into a troopship run by the American army! What a comedown, but by now it was too late to get out of it. The passenger cabins had been allocated to officers on passage, and the ship's holds had been converted to carry troops. The ship was quite unsuitable as a troopship in the tropics. There was little ventilation and the heat in the cabins was enervating even for myself who had just come from the high temperatures of Calcutta. I certainly felt some sympathy for the troops crammed in large numbers down in the airless holds of the ship. Most of the passengers were American troops and officers. There were only three or four other Naval officers besides myself, a couple of them from the Indian Navy and some Indian Army officers. I was wishing that I had stayed in Calcutta, where I would have had some control over which ship I would take passage on. Little did I know it at the time but our troubles were only starting.

Not long after boarding, we set sail for the U.K. via Suez. It was something of a relief to get to sea and away from the stifling heat of land. It was still hot on board crossing the Arabian Sea and in the Red Sea, until we got into the Mediterranean but we soon settled down to shipboard routine. I could not help comparing our conditions with those on the *Mauretania* on the way out to India. The ship was overcrowded and there was little spare room anywhere. There were no deck games, reading rooms or large dining rooms as there had been on the Cunard liner. We spent most of our time reading our own books, which passed from one to another until they had all been read. After mealtimes there was always some competition to get out on deck to secure a spot shaded from the scorching sun by a deckhouse or funnel, where one could obtain some cool from the breeze caused by the ship's forward motion.

There was a part of the boat deck which ran around the front of the bridge and overlooked the forward well deck a couple of decks below. From this vantage point one could look down to the part of the ship where the troops had their recreation area, and we were often amused by their attempts to play various games, such as football or baseball, whilst the ship was rolling in a seaway. This area was also used to serve their meals when the weather was fine. I remember watching one day when dinner was being served. A long table had been set up by the cooks on which the various dishes had been placed in a sort of buffet style. The soldiers were queuing and passing along the table from one cook to the next, collecting on their plates the different portions of food. Most of them had two plates, one for the main course and one for dessert. I noticed one large, American Negro approaching the table. He had only one plate and I wondered how he was going to cope, because he did not look like a man who would miss out on any food available. As he moved along the table he held out his plate and received a goodly portion of meat, veg and gravy, then came to the cook who was handing out the sweet, which appeared to be something like apple pie and custard. When the cook asked him for his sweet plate he said he only had the one plate and to put this sweet on the same plate as his meat and veg. The cook obliged and as he put the apple pie and custard on top of the meat and veg, commented with a grin, 'That's right, mate, you may as well mix it on deck as down in the hold!'

At the beginning of the voyage our own food, served in the officers' dining room, was reasonable enough, although not of the same standard as on the *Mauretania*. However, by the time we reached the Red Sea it became obvious that there was a serious shortage of food on board, as a number of normally essential items such as fresh meat and vegetables disappeared off the menu altogether. By the time we reached Suez most food items had gone, and we were reduced to ship's biscuits. I suppose that after my experiences of lack of food some years back in north Russia,

I was more able to cope with the shortage now encountered. In fact, ship's biscuits would have been considered something of a luxury in Murmansk. Commonly known in the Navy as 'hard tack', ship's biscuits were specially made biscuits containing vitamins and other essential food ingredients. They could be stored indefinitely and were carried by all ships as a reserve supply for when food became short. They were also carried in sealed containers in most ships' lifeboats. The biscuits were not particularly unpleasant to eat, but they were extremely hard, like dog biscuits, and one could break a tooth on them if not careful. They had one rather unpleasant fault. If they were ever used, it was usually in an emergency, after they had been stored for a long time, and they were therefore full of weevils. There was a trick for dealing with the weevils which was commonly known only by seagoing people. If the biscuit had weevil holes in it, a sharp tap on a hard surface such as the table top made the weevils drop out, and the biscuit could then be eaten without the weevils.

The Naval types on board were amused at the antics of our fellow passengers trying to get the weevils out by breaking the biscuits open into ever smaller pieces and ultimately ending with a small pile of biscuit crumbs and weevils on the table. Some of them were reluctant to follow the 'tapping' routine explained to them, in fear that they might accidentally eat a weevil hidden inside the biscuit. We explained that if this did happen it would only mean an extra bit of protein and would not do any harm! Some were not impressed, and continued breaking their biscuits into crumbs before eating them.

By this time we had passed through the Suez Canal and arrived at Port Said on the Mediterranean coast. We felt we were making headway and were nearing the final part of the voyage. We could not get going into the Mediterranean quickly enough, but our hopes were dashed for we remained at Port Said for several days. We were never told the reason for this delay, but there were lots of rumours. The most prevalent rumour was that the Captain wanted to take on fuel and food supplies but had no money to pay for them. If this was the reason we would not have been surprised, because we were not impressed by the manner in which the ship was run as a troop ship.

After a number of days of impatient waiting at Port Said we finally set sail on the last leg of our voyage to Liverpool. Some food had arrived on board, and although it was an improvement on hard tack, it left a lot to be desired. It consisted mainly of rice and vegetables. Enough to keep body and soul together but not very appetising. There was a little fresh fruit at first but it ran out long before we left the Mediterranean. We had no more stops before Liverpool, and were eager to get going.

The passage along the Med was uneventful and, apart from the food, enjoyable enough because we were now moving into a more temperate climate where, with the breeze caused by the ship's movement, the heat was much less oppressive. As we passed by Corsica, I could not help comparing my thoughts now with those on the way out. After spending some time in the tropics, the climate here felt beautifully cool and agreeable, whereas on the way out at this point we felt all but overcome by the heat, having changed into our tropical gear in the Atlantic before passing through Gibraltar. Now, on the homeward voyage, we were out of our tropical gear and into our blue uniform several days before reaching Gibraltar.

Not long after passing through the Straits of Gibraltar we were donning our blue greatcoats to protect us from what seemed an icy Atlantic wind. By the time we reached the approaches to Liverpool the rain had arrived, and the cold wet of the typical English summer drove us to the warmth of below-decks shelter. On arrival in Liverpool we wasted no time in disembarking. I was not sorry to be leaving the ship which had been my not too comfortable home for the last few weeks.

Norman Sparksman

It was now June 1946. My order for release from Naval Service required me, on arrival in the U.K., to report to Wembley football stadium in London, which at the time was being used as a release centre for service personnel being discharged from the armed forces. My release order stated: 'You have been granted 16 days' foreign service leave expiring on 19th June 1946 and 56 days' resettlement leave expiring on 14th August 1946. This meant that my Naval pay would stop in August and I would once more become a civilian.

In the meantime, after disembarking at Liverpool I lost no time making my way to Wembley Stadium, where I had never been before and knew only as the headquarters of an English football team. I was rather surprised to find that the stadium more resembled a shopping mall, with all manner of tailors and outfitting shops. It was quite interesting to be able to wander around these shops and clothe myself entirely from head to toe; suit, shirts, socks, shoes etc., all at His Majesty's expense. On entering the centre I had been given a suitcase and by the time I left it was crammed full with brand new civilian clothes. Some of the other officers were so keen to get back to civilian life they changed into their new clothes and packed their uniforms in their cases. As for myself, I remember feeling just as odd getting into civilian clothes at this point as I did all those years ago when I first donned Naval uniform. Somehow, I felt more at home in uniform and decided to wait until I reached home before making the change.

I did not linger in London. It was nearly two years since I last had any leave and I was anxious to get home. After completing my outfitting at Wembley I took a train to Stranraer in Scotland, where I caught a ferry to Larne in the north of Ireland and thence to my home in Bangor, where I received a hearty welcome from my parents. It was five years since I had gone off as a rather raw recruit to my first Naval training school in Plymouth. A lot had happened since then.

Jottings of a Young Sailor

It was an odd feeling arriving home on my last leave. I didn't have to go back after a couple of weeks. There was no more war. No more dodging bombs and rockets in London. No more wondering if a torpedo was going to dispatch you into the next world while you slept. I was now a civilian. I did not have to trot off to the other end of the world at someone's beck and call. I felt a little bit like a fish out of water. Civilian life had become an unfamiliar world to me. No doubt I would get used to it again in time.

MELROSE BOOKS

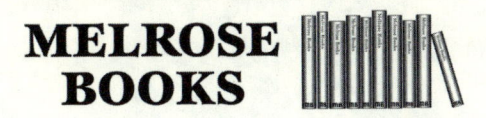

If you enjoyed this book you may also like:

That's Life In A Blue Suit
William G. Thomas

Four young men decide to dodge call up papers for National Service in 1956, by signing nine years of their young lives away in the Royal Navy, the service of their choice. The Suez War is the catalyst that creates the desire to serve in all four.

Size: 198 mm x 129 mm	Pages: 360	
Binding: B Format Paperback	ISBN: 978-1-906050-08-5	£15.99

Twenty-Two Hundred Days to Pulo We
Jack Edwards

Twenty-Two Hundred Days to Pulo We: My Education in the Navy is one of the best examples of a personal naval memoir to emerge in recent years. The author joins the Navy as an inexperienced fifteen-year-old boy and leaves over seven years later having literally grown up in the Royal Navy during WWII.

Size: 234 mm x 156 mm	Pages: 368	
Binding: Hardback	ISBN: 978-1-905226-39-9	£20.99

The Ultimate Sacrifice
David Turner

The Ultimate Sacrifice: The World War II Battleship is a revealing account of the tragedy of the sinking of the mighty battleship HMS Royal Oak told through declassified photographs and naval records, news reports of the day and statements from those who survived the horror of that fateful day.

Size: 234 mm x 156 mm	Pages: 80	
Binding: Hardback	ISBN: 978-0-954848-01-9	£11.99

The Captain's Steward
Barrie Fieldgate

Barrie Fieldgate was The Captain's Steward onboard the Royal Navy frigate HMS Broadsword, which operated in the South Atlantic during the Falklands War. As the title indicates, the core of this book comprises the observations of a Falklands War veteran during the period of that conflict.

Size: 234mm x 156 mm	Pages: 432	
Binding: Hardback	ISBN: 978-1-905226-46-7	£24.99

Guns Above, Steam Below
A.G.W. Lamont

Guns Above, Steam Below provides an insight into the lives of the people who were brought together by war and makes an insistent point about the nature of leadership. It will prove compelling reading for those with an interest in engineering, the Canadian Navy or the events of World War II.

Size: 234 mm x 156 mm	Pages: 208	
Binding: Hardback	ISBN: 978-1-905226-60-3	£14.99

St Thomas' Place, Ely, Cambridgeshire CB7 4GG, UK
www.melrosebooks.com   sales@melrosebooks.com